Gloria

ANGEL CHASERS

Discover the Truth about Angels

Bristol Publishing Company
Lubbock, TX 79414

ANGEL CHASERS

is published by
Bristol Publishing Company

Requests for information should be addressed to:
Bristol Publishing Company, Lubbock, TX 79414-2618.
You may also visit us at our website: bristolpublish.com.

ISBN: 0-9755667-0-9

Library of Congress Control Number: 2004107442

This edition printed on acid-free paper.

Unless otherwise indicated, Bible quotations are taken from The King James Version and the New International Version©1973,1978,1984 by the International Bible Society. ©1984 by Zondervan Corporation

Although the author and publishing company have made every effort to ensure the accuracy and completeness of information contained in this book, we assume no responsibility for errors, inaccuracies, omissions, or any inconsistency herein. Any slight of people, places or organizations are unintentional.

Printed in the United States of America.

ATTENTION CHURCHES, SEMINARIES, UNIVERSITIES, AND CLUBS: The author is available for speaking engagements on the subject of angels. Also, quantity discounts are available on bulk purchases of this book for educational, gift purposes, or as a premium for increasing charity or ministry contributions.

ACKNOWLEDGMENTS

I would like to thank my mother who gave me the idea to write this book and encouraged me throughout. This book was birthed with much prayer. Every time I sat in front of my computer to write, it was as if I were having my devotional time with God. "Am I writing or am I praying?" I'd ask myself. Many times the two fused together like carbon and pressure working together to produce a fine diamond. The carbon is my hands. The pressure is the Spirit of God. Thank you, God, for applying the firm pressure I needed to produce my diamond of love ANGEL CHASERS.

PREFACE

This modest work was written for those who are chasing after the truth about angels. Its purpose is *not* to turn people to angels but for the study of angels to turn people to God.

ANGEL CHASERS was also written because many people have questions about the supernatural, invisible world.

- What are angels?
- Where do they come from?
- Why are they here?
- Are they like a man, but just a little more powerful?
- How will I know when I see one?
- If one does appear what's going to happen; what should I expect?
- What is their purpose and agenda?

These questions and more are answered as we discuss God's angels, Satan's fallen angels, and demons. With so much erroneous information circulating on this subject today, let's dive deep into this ocean of confusion and see if we can swim our way into clear waters. Through ANGEL CHASERS, our understanding of angels can be clarified as we explore their origins, nature, roles, and functions. Scripture references are woven throughout this book like a golden thread holding each discussion together. The true angel stories provide real-life examples of the facts presented in this book.

This book is designed for people of all ages from eight years old to eighty. ANGEL CHASERS was written so that all could learn the truth about these wonderful beings.

CONTENTS

CHAPTER ONE

Angel Basics

ANGELS

"Take this man to prison"
The man heard Herod say
And then four squads of soldiers
Came and carried him away.

Chained up between two watchmen
Peter tried to sleep
But beyond the walls an endless
Prayer was lifted for his keep.

Then light cut through the darkness
Of a lonely prison cell
And the chains that bound the man of
God opened up and fell

And running to his people
Before the break of day
There was only one thing on his mind
Only one thing to say,
Angels watching over me
Every move I make
Angels watching over me
Every step I take.

ANGEL CHASERS

God only knows the times my life
Was threatened and today
A reckless car ran out of gas
Before it came my way.

Near misses all around me,
Accidents unknown
Though I never see with human eyes
The hands that lead me home.
God, I know they're all around me
All day and through the night.

When the enemy is closing in
I know sometimes they fight
To keep my feet from falling
I'll never turn away.

If you're asking what's protecting me
Then you're gonna hear me say
Angels watching over me
Every move I make
Angels watching over me
Every step I take
Angels watching over me
Though I never see with human eyes
The hands that lead me home.

Amy Grant, Straight Ahead, *1984*

The lyrics to this song sum up the essence of angelic relationships with the human race. They guard us, direct us, comfort us, dress us, and lead us home to heaven. "Angels Watching Over Me" has been the theme song of millions since the beginning of man. There has never been a time on the earth when angels weren't here. God's flames of fire—his ministering servants—are ready, willing and able to shower the message of God's love and compassion on us.

Let me share two stories about angels who bring messages of God's exceedingly great love, and his desire for us to have peace, hope, comfort, and rest. These two things are the "angel basics" for all their workings in our lives. The first story was told by Eva Stealey of Baltimore, Maryland.

Peace be still . . .

Shortly after I had my second baby, I was numb from the epidural and didn't realize how heavily I was bleeding. A student nurse by the name of Julie came in to check on me. She said, "That's not normal. I'm calling my instructor to look at you."

I was frightened after her visit, all alone and bleeding. Julie returned with an older woman and they quickly took control of the situation. As they were leaving they said, "Everything's fine. Just rest now so you can regain your strength and take care of your beautiful son."

I drifted off into a peaceful sleep and was awakened a little while later by a nurse who had come in to change my dressing. "Julie just changed it," I told her. "She's one of the student nurses. She was here with her instructor."

She gazed at me as though I had lost my mind. "There's nobody named Julie on this shift," she said. "And this isn't a teaching hospital. We have no students and no instructors."

It took me a minute to realize that what I experienced was a blessed visit by a heavenly spirit from a God who cared enough about my concerns to send me a message of comfort and hope. Thank you, Lord. Thank you, angels.

The second story, entitled "Out and Cold," was

shared by Pamela Medford, who lives in British Columbia, Canada. Although the next story happened twenty-five years ago, the author said she recalled the incident as though it were yesterday. At one of the lowest moments of her life, a compassionate God looked down from heaven, saw her tears, and sent his messenger to give her hope for the future.

Come unto me all who are weary and burdened . . .

My daughter, Jessica, was about a year old. I was a single mom and dirt poor. In order to get some money to pay for food, I had to walk many miles in deep snow. I had a cheap pair of boots on and got a blister as I was walking. I didn't have gloves or a warm coat.

As you can imagine, I was miserable and upset. I cried and the tears froze on my lashes. I couldn't believe this was happening to me.

I made it to my destination, got the money, and was able to take the bus home. The bus stop was out in the open and there wasn't anyone around except an elderly man sitting quietly on the bench, which was very dry when it should have been wet.

I sat down next to him. He smiled at me. His smile was so radiant that I felt warm and at ease. I can't remember much about our conversation except his asking about my daughter. I showed him a photo of her and he said, "She'll be very successful." Then he told me my blister would be better real soon.

"How do you know about that?" I asked.

He just smiled and said, "Everything will be okay."

The bus came around the corner and I called out to him, "The bus is here," but he was gone. There hadn't been time for him to go anywhere since, as I said, the area was wide open with no buildings around. I was shocked. All the way home all I could think of was that I'd been visited by an angel.

When I got home, the blister was gone and my daughter is now doing very well just as he predicted!

What is an angel?

To put it simply, an angel is a heavenly being used by God to bring messages to mankind (*The Basic Bible Dictionary*). The term *angel* comes from the Greek *angelos*, which means messenger. In Persian, *angaros* means courier. In Hebrew, the term is *malakh*, which also means messenger. The name refers to the angels' primary duty to shuttle back and forth between heaven and earth, bringing God's answers to prayers to people on the earth. These answers to prayers may include many things, from a prayer to make a sick child well to a prayer for rescue from harm's way. Angels also have a key role in assisting and protecting on the earth and on our journey to heaven when we die.

Besides answering prayers, angels have their own culture, just as we have many different cultures on the earth. The *American Heritage Dictionary* defines a culture as a behavior pattern, belief system, institution, and all other products of thought, especially as expressed in a particular community or period. The culture of God's angels expresses God's loving, kind, generous behavior and belief system. In other words, God's angels act godly and speak the words they receive from God. God is the focus of their life.

Their number-one priority is God and doing what God wants. God's kids are number two. God affects the way angels do everything. So if we see angels acting or speaking contrary to God's word as written in the Bible, they are not godly angels, but Satan's evil angels.

Why did God create angels?

Why would God create angels when he certainly doesn't need them? John Calvin, in his *Institutes of the*

Christian Religion, written in 1536-1559, translated by Henry Beveridge, 1845-1846, summarizes my thoughts exactly on this matter:

> In creating angels, God must have had our interests in mind. God employs angels simply as a help to our weakness, in order to raise our hopes or strengthen our confidence. Calvin goes on to say if God in his goodness and indulgence chooses to provide angels for our weakness, it would ill-become us to overlook the favor.

His conclusions seem to reflect Hebrews 1:14, that says angels are "ministering spirits sent to serve [or minister to] those who will inherit salvation." In other words, angels are here for us—God's kids.

Even though they are here for us, they are not under our direct command. This seems to be true, because angels are not mentioned in the creation account in Genesis 1 where God tells man to have dominion over a list of things. This omission might indicate that angels are not under human authority but that they take their orders straight from the throne of God. During creation week God gave man authority over many beings, but not angels. In other words, even though they were created to minister to us or to serve us, we can't order them to wash our clothes or take out the garbage or find our keys.

Where do angels come from?

First of all, angels are created beings. God made angels. In Colossians 1:16 we read that "all things were created" by Jesus Christ. Christ caused all things to come into being for his purpose and pleasure. Some might say that Paul wasn't talking about angels. But evidently he was because later on he said, ". . . *things in heaven and on earth*, visible and invisible, whether thrones or powers or rulers or authorities, all things were created by him [by Christ], and for him." Paul seems to be extra careful to include things in heaven and earth, which certainly seem to include the angels.

Finally, when they are worshiping God in Revelation 4, the angels themselves declare that the Lord created them, "They laid their crowns before the throne and said, You are worthy, our Lord and God, to receive glory and honor and power, for you created all things, and by your will they were created and have their being." Not only does this express the angels' thought of God having created them, but they also confirm that it is by him that they have continued existence—"have their being."

The creation of angels

In this section we are not attempting to describe how angels were created, but to provide a biblical account of their arrival on the scene. In general, angels were created at some point before the earth was formed. In Job 38:4 the Lord told Job that the angels had already been created before the earth was formed, and were there celebrating at that event. God asks Job, "Where were you when I laid the earth's foundation?" Then he describes still more of what was happening when the earth was created, "The morning stars [angels] sang together, and the sons of God [angels] shouted for joy" (Job 38:7). Therefore, it seems angels were made before the third day of creation when God gathered the waters into seas and the dry land appeared as mentioned in Genesis 1:9-10). If angels were partying and celebrating when the earth was created, they had to be here before the earth and man.

Psalm 104 seems to reflect the same ordering of the angelic creation. It first mentions the light, then the heavens and the gathering of heavenly waters or clouds, angels or flames of fire, then the land, seas, animals, and man. In this Psalm the angels are mentioned right before the mention of earth in verse 5:

> Bless the Lord, O my soul. O Lord my God, thou art very great; thou art clothed with honor and majesty. Who covers thyself with light as with a garment: who stretches out the heavens like a curtain. Who lays the beams of his chambers in the waters: who maketh the clouds his chariot: who walketh upon the wings of the wind. Who maketh his angels spirits; his ministers a flaming fire. Who laid the foundations of the earth, that it should not be removed forever.

To find the answer to when angels were created and where angels come from, we have to look at the creation account. Here we do not find a specific answer such as God said, "Let us create angels and then they were." But by looking at the pieces of the puzzle of the creation account found in several parts of the Bible, we see that the angels were created sometime prior to the formation of the earth.

Conclusions

Angels are wonderful creatures of God. They were created to be his servants who do his will, to assist and protect us and to bring answers to our prayers. They are also God's press agents in that they relay God's messages to us. They have no messages of their own. The angels sang before the earth became, and because they were created before us and were not in the Genesis 1 list of things for man to have dominion over, we have no authority over them. During the earth's creation, their role was not to assist God in its formation but to rejoice with him in its creation.

Chapter Two

The Different Kinds of Angels

Angels, archangels, cherubim and seraphim, the living creatures, powers, and principalities—these are just some of the angelic beings mentioned in the Bible. Are there really different kinds of angels, or is this just their job description?

One truck driver on the lonely road home—Paul Spencer of Clinton, Michigan—is given a look into the spirit realm and discovers just how many different kinds of angels there are. He finds some of them exotic to the eye. Here's his story.

And the angels numbered thousands upon thousands . . .

I was on my way home from a week on the road, driving my rig back to Michigan. It was midweek but I had planned to stop at the Hegwish Baptist Church in northwestern Indiana.

Near as I can recall, it was the first week of April 1979. I arrived about an hour before the service began. I parked my truck on the side of the church and was waiting patiently when a big fellow, who turned out to be the pastor, asked if I wanted a tour of the church. It was quite lovely, as far as churches go.

When the service began, I sat in the rear left of the sanctuary about three pews from the back so I could see everything. The congregation sang a few hymns and a few songs of praise. Then Pastor Winn Worley said: "We're going to call in the angels. They overcame the Devil by the blood of the Lamb, Jesus, by the word of their testimony and loved not their lives even unto death."

And that's when it happened. To this very day, it's the most absolutely incredible thing I have ever witnessed. Waves of loving kindness washed over me. Warm compassionate feelings filled the room, reverberating from the floor to the ceiling.

Glancing from side to side around the room, I sat in utter silence, tears of joy rolling down my cheeks, totally engulfed in a depth of love that I had never believed possible.

There were angels standing shoulder to shoulder down each wall and across the back. There were angels behind the pulpit; mighty men, mature, strong, well built. Some had blonde hair, others brown or sandy colored. Their eyes looked straight through you from kindly calm faces. They were dressed in togas of pure white with large leather belts and high gold or silver buckles and calf-high sandals.

Directly to the pastor's right and left were two cherubim, with wings that were snow white and fluffy and soft. They hovered in place—as though they were ministering to the pastor.

And then I saw wheels of angels hovering above. They were seraphim. I believe, seven of them comprising a ring. They all had six wings but they didn't flap. They just sprouted off to each side and the wings of another. For lack of a better term, they looked like a shiny chrome mag wheel. Several of these rings moved around the space between our heads and the ceiling. These angels had auras of gold while the others had halos of silver.

The Bible tells us that we are not to worship angels—that they are God's messengers. Since that night in Indiana so many years ago, I have seen angels a few more times, but none of my later encounters could compare to that one.

This man was allowed a view into the spirit realm that many would love to feel and see. Oh, by the way, those angels he described looking like a "mag wheel" are found in Isaiah's description of the seraphim listed below. They cover their face with two wings, cover their feet with two wings, and then stand and fly together in one accord or one circle with the other two wings. So think about it. They would sort of look like a "mag wheel!"

Seraphim

The name *seraph* means "burning one" or "shining one," reminding us that God makes his angels "flames of fire" (Psalm 104:4; Hebrews 1:7). The seraphim dwell so close to the presence of God that they burn with holy brilliance.

They are mentioned by name in only one passage in the Bible, but it is a magnificent scene. The prophet Isaiah in a vision sees God on his throne and hears voices around him crying out enthusiastically. Isaiah 6:1-4 describes the seraphim's activity and how they sound out a continual praise to God:

> In the year that king Uzziah died, I saw also the Lord sitting upon a throne, high and lifted up, and his train filled the temple. Above it stood the seraphim: each one had six wings; with twain he covered his face, and with twain he covered his feet, and with twain he did fly. And one cried unto another, and said, Holy, holy, holy, is the LORD of hosts: the

> whole earth is full of his glory. And the posts
> of the door moved at the voice of him that
> cried, and the house was filled with smoke.

I believe this graphic scene of the seraphim may say more than what is noticed at first glance. The six-winged seraphs use two of their wings to cover their face to protect themselves from the brilliance of God's glory when they're in his presence. With the two other wings they cover their feet. This speaks of their humility and reverence in waiting for God's direction. With the last two wings they propel themselves speedily to do God's will. Like Ezekiel's vision of the cherubim, Isaiah's vision of the seraphim provides another picture of reverence and adoring awe to help us in approaching our heavenly Father.

In his tape series, "War in the Heavenlies," Benny Hinn gives some insight as to why the seraphim were so enthusiastic in their praise of God in Isaiah 6:1-4:

> When the seraphim look at themselves and
> say, "Holy, holy, holy," the posts of the doors
> of heaven move in response to their voices.
> They continually talk about God's glory, be-
> cause every time they look at God, they
> would see another revelation of God's glory,
> his might, his power, his holiness.

God's glory deals with who he is—his attributes. When God revealed himself to Moses in Exodus 34, Moses richly proclaimed some of God's attributes. When any being is in the presence of God, his response is to what he sees. If you and I were on a beautiful beach in the tropics, the first thing out of our mouths would be, "This is gorgeous weather, turquoise water, white sand, refreshing tropical drink, a gentle breeze, swaying palm trees." This is why these angels respond to God's glory by crying out, "Holy, holy, holy." They're responding to the holiness they see in God.

Cherubim

The background of the cherubim is something of a mystery. Some scholars suggest that their name is related to words meaning "intercessor" or "guardian." Others see a connection to words meaning "to grasp or hold fast," or "to plow or till the ground," or "to be diligent." According to the Bible, they are majestic and beautiful. Their majesty, strength, and guardian role can be seen in the book of Genesis (3:24), where they are portrayed as mighty guardian figures like the ones who guarded the entrance of the Garden of Eden to keep Adam and Eve away from the tree of life. In Psalm 18:10, God rides upon a cherub. Perhaps cherubim (the Hebrew plural of *cherub*) are the real workhorses to the King, and they certainly should not be mistaken for the naked Valentine babies the world envisions them to be.

We do know, however, that the name *cherubim* originated in Assyria and is derived from the word *karibu*, which means "one who prays" (Constance Briggs, *Encyclopedia of Angels*). As we shall soon see, they are said to praise God day and night continuously.

Cherubim are also sometimes called "living creatures, winged creatures, and Holy Beasts, such as those found in the book of Ezekiel. We now know from the prophet Ezekiel that their primary role seems to be one of worship. Even when one looks at Satan, a former cherub, we see that he was once one of the chief praise and worship leaders in heaven, before he was kicked out for mutiny.

According to Ezekiel, cherubim are brilliant, mighty angels who signify the angelic presence around God's throne. Their role in the praise and worship of God certainly seems to be true if we look at their description found in Ezekiel 1:5-14:

> Out of the midst thereof came the likeness of four living creatures. And this was their ap-

pearance; they had the likeness of a man. And every one had four faces, and every one had four wings. And their feet were straight feet; and the sole of their feet was like the sole of a calf's foot: and they sparkled like the color of burnished brass. And they had the hands of a man under their wings on their four sides; and they four had their faces and their wings. Their wings were joined one to another; they turned not when they went; they went every one straight forward. As for the likeness of their faces, they four had the face of a man, and the face of a lion, on the right side: and they four had the face of an ox and a face of an eagle on the left side. Thus were their faces: and their wings were stretched upward; two wings of every one were joined one to another, and two covered their bodies. And they went every one straight forward: Whither the spirit was to go, they went; and they turned not when they went.

As for the likeness of the living creatures, their appearance was like burning coals of fire, and like the appearance of lamps: it went up and down among the living creatures; and the fire was bright, and out of the fire went forth lightning. And the living creatures ran and returned as the appearance of a flash of lightning.

In these verses Ezekiel describes how they sparkled like the color of burnished brass. They sparkled like this because they had been in the presence of God. Remember what Jesus looked like in the book of Revelation where it declares the same thing about him, that his feet looked like shining brass because he had been in the presence of God?

These angels shine and sparkle because they continually stand in the very presence of God. When this description talks about how their faces and wings were stretched upward, they were worshiping God. When Ezekiel describes how two of their wings were joined one with another to cover their body, they were worshiping God. Remember Satan was once connected to God's presence, worship, and protecting the very throne of heaven, walking up and down in midst of stones of fire. That's why the cherubim feet sparkle, because they are walking up and down the stones of fire in front of God's throne.

They don't just walk wherever they want to. They are led by the Spirit of God all the time. Cherubs are involved with the works of the Spirit in heaven, not on earth. The cherubim's job has to do with God's glory or with who he is. To sum it up, the cherubim are connected to the worship of God and presence of God. As I heard one wise man say, "Cherubs are cheer'er-uppers"—of the Most High God, that is.

Living Creatures

Their name—living creatures—quickly tells us that they have life and that they are created beings. The living creatures mentioned in Revelation 4 have similarities to both cherubs and seraphs. Like the cherubim mentioned in Ezekiel 1, there are four living creatures mentioned in Revelation 4:6-9. One creature has the likeness of a lion, one of an ox, one of a man, and the last one had a face of an eagle:

> And before the throne there was a sea of glass like unto crystal: and in the midst of the throne, and round about the throne, were four beasts full of eyes before and behind. And the first beast was like a lion, and the second beast like a calf, and the third beast had a face

as a man, and the fourth beast was like a flying eagle. And the four beasts had each of them six wings about him; and they were full of eyes within: and they rest not day and night, saying, Holy, holy, holy, Lord God Almighty, which was, and is, and is to come. And those beasts give glory and honor and thanks to him that sat on the throne, who liveth forever and ever, for thou hast created all things, and for thy pleasure they are and were created.

The difference between the angels mentioned in Revelation 4 and the cherubim of Ezekiel 1 is that Ezekiel's living creatures have four faces and four wings. The Revelation 4 living creatures are full of eyes and have one face.In addition, like the seraphim mentioned in Isaiah 6, they have six wings, and honor God with their continual praise of "Holy, holy, holy is the Lord God Almighty"—to which the Revelation 4 living creatures added a new phrase: "who was, and is, and is to come" (4:8). Another difference between the seraphim and the living creatures in Revelation is that the seraphim are looking at each other as they say, "He's holy, holy, holy." The living creatures were speaking to God himself, saying, "Holy, holy, holy is the Lord God Almighty."

The seraphim also differ from the living creatures in that they do not seem to live continually in the presence of God and in that they cover their faces with two of their wings as they fly by God as if to protect themselves from the brilliance of God's glory (Ezekiel 1). The living creatures, however, live "in the midst of the throne and round about the throne"(Revelation 4:6). Because they live in such close proximity to the throne of God, they may be perhaps closer to God than any other angelic being.

These angels of Revelation 4 are so close to God that they seem to be actually connected to the presence of

God. In a way that can only be described spiritually, they are so focused on God that they seem to be over-whelmed—so moved by God's presence that it literally causes them to cry out to God himself saying, "Holy, holy, holy is the Lord God Almighty." They appear to be totally lost in the worship of God, and all their eyes are so focused on him that I believe they are actually seeing with their eyes who he was, who he is, and that he is to come. God's presence so moves them that they can't help themselves. They just keep worshiping God, and they "rest not day or night" (4:8).

They have eyes in front and behind, and this tells us something else about them. They are the angels of revelation—God's revelation. We don't know everything about them, but we do know that they reveal who God is—holy. Perhaps with their eyes in front and back, like the cherubin's wheels in Ezekiel 1, they are able to see that God was, God is, and that God—Jesus is to come!

These four living creatures are not only involved in worshiping and revealing to us who God is, but are also involved in bringing about his final wrath upon the earth. In Revelation 6:1-2, the apostle John, watching Christ opening the first of the seven seals, said:

> And I saw when the Lamb opened one of the seals, and I heard, as it were the noise of thunder, one of the four beasts saying, "Come and see." And I saw, and behold a white horse: and he that sat on him had a bow; and a crown was given unto him: and he went forth conquering, and to conquer.

As Christ opens the next three seals, the other three creatures each in turn also call out, "Come!" Again their simple command immediately brings forth a horse and rider seeking to destroy the earth. These living creatures' words are few but they are powerful.

Twenty-four Elders

In close proximity to the living creatures are the twenty-four elders. When the apostle John first sees them in Revelation, they are seated on twenty-four thrones that encircle God's throne. "They are dressed in white and have crowns of gold on their heads" (4:4). These elders in Revelation are involved in proclaiming God's saving acts toward men. One of their most glorious moments is when the seventh angel sounds his trumpet in Revelation 11:15-17, JBP:

> And the seventh angel sounded; and there were great voices in heaven, saying, "The kingdoms of this world are become the kingdoms of our Lord, and of his Christ; and he shall reign for ever and ever." And the four and twenty elders, which sat before God on their seats, fell upon their faces, and worshiped God, saying, "We give thee thanks, O Lord God Almighty, which is, and was, and is to come; because thou hast taken to thee thy great power, and hast reigned."

Like the elders in the church today, they are the ones we should look up to as role models for godly behavior. Perhaps their worship and service to God is meant to be an example to those in church leadership today.

Archangels

There are three archangels mentioned in the Bible: Gabriel, Michael, and Lucifer who fell. Gabriel and Michael continue to serve the Lord, but Satan was kicked out of heaven along with his cohorts for mutiny against God. While the Bible does not mention Gabriel specifically as being an archangel, it does mention and discuss him as if he is on the same level as Michael and Lucifer, but their roles are just different. As we will see, Michael is mainly an archangel of war, Gabriel is an announcer of things to come, and Lucifer, before his fall, was the praise and worship leader of heaven. The archangels seem to be generals in the Lord's army and are singled out from the common angels as if they were of a special class possessing special powers needed to do their particular job.

1. Gabriel

Gabriel's name means "Mighty One of God." Gabriel is one of the most admired angels of all. He always seems to be bringing good and important news. He told Zechariah that he would have a son, and not just any son, but John the Baptist who would be the forerunner of Jesus (Luke 1:19). Just a little while later, he announced to Mary that she would have a son, and that he would be great and called the Son of God, and that he would reign forever and his kingdom would have no end (1:26-37). And again Gabriel brought good news in Daniel 9:21-23 when he said, "As soon as you began to pray, an answer was given."

In addition, when Jesus returns to the earth a second time to snatch away his bride, the church, 1 Thessalonians 4:16 tells us, "The Lord himself shall descend from heaven with a shout, with the voice of the archangel, and with the trump of God." Just as Gabriel announced all the past important events relative to Jesus Christ, he will probably be the one who shouts with a loud voice, "He's coming, and he's coming now. See him now, Lord of lords and King of kings, Jesus Christ, the Messiah," and the trumpets will be blaring. It will put to shame the most lavish royal procession of any king on this planet.

As Gabriel is announcing Jesus' return, I believe the fireworks will be flaring, music playing, and, as if the sky were a large video screen, the Lord's descent will be seen by every human on this earth. It seems that anything to do with the kingdom of Christ involves Gabriel.

So why does Gabriel always seem to have good news to give? Because he stays in the right place to learn it. "I am Gabriel. I stand in the presence of God" (Luke 1:19).

2. Michael

The second archangel mentioned in the Bible is Michael. His name means, "Who is like God?" While Gabriel is more of an announcing and preaching angel, Michael is more involved in warfare and protection. The angel Michael is mentioned five times in Scripture (there are other Michaels, but they are not angels).

In the Old Testament, Michael is a royal champion of God's people Israel. He is referred to three times in Daniel, and his title gets progressively more exalted and personal toward Israel. First he's called "one of the chief princes" in Daniel 10:13 when he comes to the aid of Gabriel who is fighting the evil angels of Satan to get a message from God through to Daniel, the prophet of God's people Israel. Then it's "Michael, your prince" in Daniel 10:21, again speaking of Michael's coming to the aid of Gabriel in the fight against the princes of darkness. Finally it's "Michael, the great prince who protects your people" in Daniel 12:1.

In the New Testament, Michael is mentioned twice, in Jude and in Revelation. In Jude 9 he's called "the archangel Michael." This particular "archangel" means the angel who is "first, principal, or chief." Here Michael gives us a lesson on how to fight the devil in his fight with Satan over the body of Moses, the great leader who led Israel out of the bondage and slavery of Egypt. He didn't fight the devil in his own strength. Instead, Michael said, "The Lord rebukes [or stops] you." We should be like Michael and speak the word and let Jesus, the Lord, stop the devil's attack against us.

In Revelation 12:7 Michael is in command of the God's warriors in the great heavenly battle against

Satan. "And there was war in heaven. Michael and his angels fought against the dragon, and the dragon and his angels fought back." And as one would guess, God's angels win.

So, even though Michael's name means "who is like God?" the answer, of course, is that no one compares to God. So no matter how great Michael or other angels are, our praise goes only to God, "who alone does marvelous deeds" (Psalm 72:18).

3. Former Archangel Lucifer a.k.a. Satan

Concerning the third archangel mentioned in the Bible, Lucifer, we look at the five "I wills" found in Isaiah 14:4-18, in order to fully understand his personality, method of operation, and goals. All theology scholars will agree that this section of Isaiah is talking about the literal and historical destruction of Babylon, but it also is a picture of the fall of Lucifer. Verses 4 - 12 present a picture of Satan's personality, and verses 13 and 14 present the famous five "I will" statements which reflect the cause of his fall.

a. Lucifer's personality

Verse 4: "That thou shall take up this proverb against the king of Babylon, and say, How hath the oppressor ceased! The golden city ceased!" The king of Babylon is also a picture or representation of the antichrist—the devil, Satan or Lucifer, who is against Jesus Christ.

Verse 5: "The LORD hath broken the staff of the wicked, and the sceptre of the rulers." The Lord brought Lucifer down like a lightning bolt falling from the sky (Luke 10:18).

Verse 6: "He who smote the people in wrath with a continual stroke, he that ruled the nations in anger, is persecuted, and none hinders." Satan hates us and has no use for us unless we help him propagate his agenda. He is a thief who comes to kill, steal, and destroy us (John 10:10).

Verses 7-8: "The whole earth is at rest, and is quiet: they break forth into singing. Yea, the fir trees rejoice at thee, and the cedars of Lebanon, saying, Since thou art laid down, no feller is come up against us." I believe this is a prophetic view of how the earth will be when Satan is gone.

Verse 9: "Hell from beneath is moved for thee to meet thee at thy coming: it stirred up the dead for thee, even all the chief ones of the earth; it hath raised up from their thrones all the kings of the nations." Hell was prepared for Lucifer, his evil angels, and the demons, who participated in the mutiny against God. Hell was not prepared for mankind. But a person who rejects God and chooses Satan as his lord will go with him to hell and spend eternal life with his or her lord, Satan. Children of God will go to heaven and spend eternal life with their God.

Verses 10-11: "All they shall speak and say unto thee, Art thou also become weak as we? Art thou become like unto us? Thy pomp is brought down to the grave, and the noise of thy violence: the worm is spread under thee, and the worms cover thee." I can just hear the demons (see pre-Adamic race theory in Chapter Six) saying, "If God sent us here and he sent you (Satan) here, then you must be as weak as we are. You are not God. O what fools we've been." If we could be a fly on the walls of hell, surely this would be the response we would hear from the fallen inhabitants of the earth to Satan.

Verse 12: "How art thou fallen from heaven, O Lucifer, son of the morning! how art thou cut down to the ground, which didst weaken the nations!" Lucifer, the former "light holder," was in heaven at one time. Lucifer or Satan went from being one of the most powerful angels in heaven and on the earth to nothing. He had the God-given gift of leading others to God. Satan chose to use this gift to turn some of the angels of heaven and the inhabitants of the earth to himself. He cheapened his God-given leadership skills when he led by deception. What he was to use for good, Satan used for evil. He was and is the master of deception. He convinced a third of the angels in heaven that he was like God, and they were cast out of heaven with him. Revelation 12:3-4 seems to confirm this as it describes how a third of heavens angels fell with Satan. The New Living Translation reads this way:

> Suddenly, I witnessed in heaven another significant event. I saw a large red dragon [which is defined later in verse 9 as Satan] with seven heads and ten horns, with seven crowns on his heads. His tail dragged down one-third of the stars [the common Bible name for angels], which he threw to earth.

In addition, I believe he also turned the nations on the earth at that time against God and toward himself. He was God's praise and worship leader, but instead he kept the praise and worship for himself. It is better never to have gained a high position than to have gained it, tasted it, and then lost it. When this happens, the fallen person continually tries to get back to where he was and is driven to this pursuit and will settle for nothing less than that. So it is with Satan. After he fell, he came back to the Garden of Eden seeking to regain his position of earthly authority that God had given to Adam. He knew that if he went directly to Adam, he would kick him out. So he went through Eve and fooled her into disobeying God and obeying him, thus giving him back the authority over the earth that he once had. He is still not satisfied with that. He wants to be like the Most High God. As we see in the book of Revelation, his end shall be in the lake of fire forever and ever.

b. Cause of the fall of Lucifer

Verse 13: "For thou hast said in thine heart, I will ascend into heaven, I will exalt my throne above the stars of God: I will sit also upon the mount of the congregation, in the sides of the north." Satan was looking up from the earth and saw himself in heaven on a throne above God. He did not want to be an angel under the authority of God. He wanted to be over God. In other words, he wanted to be in charge of God, the heavenly angels, and the host or congregation of beings in the earth.

Verse 14: "I will ascend above the heights of the clouds; I will be like the most High." This epitomizes Satan's ultimate goal to be like God. He wanted total control of everyone and everything. Here he shows his true motive—to be God.

Verse 15: "Yet thou shall be brought down to hell, to the sides of the pit." Because of his rebellion, mutiny, and prideful criminal activity, Satan is sent to hell.

Verse 16: "They that see thee shall narrowly look upon thee, and consider thee, saying, Is this the man that made the earth to tremble, that did shake kingdoms." Demons, the pre-Adamic inhabitants of the earth, stared at him, probably shaking their heads as they said, "Is this the one we lost the glory of God over? He isn't all that great!"

c. The fall of Lucifer

Ezekiel 28 provides us with a vivid description of Lucifer and his fall. Before the fall, Lucifer was God's anointed cherub, archangel, and praise and worship leader. Before the fall you will see the Bible calling Satan Lucifer, which means "light bearer." After the fall his name was changed to Satan or the devil, which represents the ultimate in darkness.

Verse 12 talks about the "king of Tyre," which is Satan. I believe he was in charge of God's pre-Adamic

Eden, and verse 13 seems to confirm this when it says, "Thou hast been in Eden, the garden of God." The Adamic Eden described in Genesis 1 belonged to Adam.

Verse 13 provides a graphic description of Lucifer before the fall:

> Every precious stone was thy covering, the sardius, topaz, and the diamond, the beryl, the onyx, and the jasper, the sapphire, the emerald, and the carbuncle, and gold: the workmanship of thy tabrets and of thy pipes was prepared in thee in the day that thou wast created.

In other words, Lucifer was covered with jewels, and created with musical instruments within his being. He was in charge of the praise and worship team in heaven, and when he opened his mouth, an orchestra sang. He had two positions, archangel and cherub, which is unusual. The only being in heaven with more than one office is Jesus the Christ. Lucifer was next in position to the Godhead. He was honored above all other angels. No other angel had two positions.

Verse 14 further describes Lucifer, "Thou art the anointed cherub that covereth; and I have set thee so: thou wast upon the holy mountain of God; thou hast walked up and down in the midst of the stones of fire." Here it says he was anointed by God and was allowed upon the holy mountain of God (the government or kingdom of God), and even walked up and down midst of stones of fire in front of the throne of God. These stones were lit up with God's glory. Lucifer walked up and down the stones of God, singing onto the Lord. His job was chief worshiper of the Godhead—Father, Son-Jesus, and the Holy Spirit.

Verses 16 and 17 describe how Lucifer sinned and was cast out of the mountain of God:

> By the multitude of thy merchandise [posi-

tion and power] they have filled the midst of thee with violence, and thou hast sinned: therefore I will cast thee as profane out of the mountain of God: and I will destroy thee, O covering cherub, from the midst of the stones of fire. Thine heart was lifted up because of thy beauty [pride], thou hast corrupted thy wisdom by reason of thy brightness: I will cast thee to the ground, I will lay thee before kings, that they may behold thee.

Remember when Isaiah 14:16 said the inhabitants of the earth at the time looked hard at him and said, "Is this the one who fooled the nations?" This was all pre-Adamic. There were kings on the earth. There were cities. There was life on the earth before Adam.

Verse 18 describes the enormity of the sin and why God reacted so violently to it, "Thou hast defiled thy sanctuaries by the multitude of thine iniquity." Lucifer corrupted God's word to the inhabitants of the earth at that time, and kept God's worship to himself rather than giving God's worship to the earth. He kept it himself and turned everyone on the earth against God.

If he could turn the whole earth against God, maybe now you can better understand why we need the Holy Spirit (see Chapter Six: Demons, the race on the earth before Adam, Proof 4) in us to assist and protect us. If God only gave us the angels to protect us, we'd be dead. We need more than the angels. We need what the blood of Jesus purchased (forgiveness of sin, victory in this life, and eternal life) and the Holy Spirit.

So, if Verse 17 describes how Satan was cast to the ground, what's he doing in the second heaven today? After deceiving Adam and Eve in the Garden of Eden, Adam gave him what he had been given by God—command over the Earth. People ask, "Why did God let September 11 happen?" It is because, as the Bible says,

"Satan is the god of this world" (2 Corinthians 4:4).

d. Effect of Lucifer's fall on the earth

God gave Adam authority over the earth and everything in it. When Adam bowed his knee to Satan in the Garden of Eden, he gave his God-given authority to Satan to rule over the earth, and sin came into the world. Jesus took back this authority when he lived a sinless life, died on the cross in our place for our sins, and arose from the dead with the keys to the authority over the earth in his hands.

Jesus has done his part to give us back our authority over the earth and everything in it, but unless we pray in the name of Jesus and take back that authority, Satan, who is a thief, will continue to rule over us. Satan was ruling in those people who flew into those buildings on September 11. They gave him permission to function in the earth in that way. God had nothing to do with that evil.

e. Where are Satan, his evil angels, and demons today?

After being kicked out of heaven, Satan came to the Garden of Eden and deceived Adam and Eve, and the earth came under his rule again. Everything Satan had lost when he fell, he has regained. Satan and the evil angels are back in power. Where are the demons? They are still in the pit or hell. The other evil angels who slept with women to pollute Adam's pure seed or offspring and stop the coming Messiah, Jesus Christ (as we shall see momentarily) are in a special place in hell called Tartarus. Satan and the other evil angels live in the second heaven (Ephesians 6).

But before we go any further, we need to clarify all these heavens. The first heaven is the atmosphere. The second heaven, as previously mentioned, is where Satan and some of the evil angels live.

Speaking of evil angels in the second heaven, in Daniel 10 an angel tells the man of God that he set out to bring the answer to his prayer the day he prayed it, but the "Prince of Persia," an evil angel, delayed him for almost a month until archangel Michael came and helped him to get through. The Prince of Persia is commonly thought to be one of those "powers and principalities in the heavenly realm" (Ephesians 6) assigned to the country of Persia.

Evil angels can control regions or an entire country. The following is a true story but with a little twist. God assigned his angel over the city of Los Angeles probably to counter some evil force assigned there. According to Click on WalkThroughLife.com (November 8, 2000), this is what happened:

Angel Over the City

I left my room and decided to go stand outside on the upper porch and look out over the city of Los Angeles as I often did at the time. It was 1986. To my amazement I witnessed a large figure of what I understood to be an angel, but it was enshrouded by clouds. To my eyes there were no other clouds out that afternoon. His face wasn't visible (I took this to mean humility before God), he had wings, there was a rainbow around his head, and he was standing on a cloud that appeared to have flashing fire within it. There was a large sickle in his hands as if he were set to reap. I don't know to this day what the angel was going to do or why, but I felt it necessary to pray for the people of that city.

Evil angels are powerful, but God's angels are ultimately more powerful because they receive their power from the Lord God Almighty.

Going back to the explanations of the three heavens—the first heaven is the atmosphere, the second heaven is where the evil angels live, and finally, the third heaven is where God lives. Mankind lives on the earth. And Philippians 2:10 speaks of "things under the earth." Who is under the earth? There are five inhabited worlds below us.

Five Worlds Below the Earth

1. Sheol

The first world is called *Sheol*. This word is Hebrew for hell. According to the Bible, this hell is the place where all unrighteous souls go. It is a place of torment and fire as described in Deuteronomy 32:22. Here it is called the "lowest hell." This shows us that there are various sections of hell. Isaiah 38:10 talks about the "gates of my grave." In other words, hell has gates. Isaiah 38:10 also says that hell deprives us of "the residue of our years." Hell takes people before their time.

Job 21:13 provides a description of how fast we go from physical death to either heaven or hell. Job 21:13 says that we go to heaven or hell "in a moment to the grave." This shows there is no time period before we go to hell. Just as 2 Corinthians 5:8 says for the Christian believer to be absent from the body is to be present in the Lord. For the unbeliever, to be absent from the body is to be instantly present in hell.

Sadly, once the wicked go to hell, they don't like it there and try to keep other family members from coming, as seen in Luke 16:19 where Jesus tells us the story of a wicked rich man who called up to heaven to send someone to tell his brothers not to live in such a way as to cause them to go to hell.

2. Paradise

This is a place where the Old Testament saints were

held, before Jesus, the Savior and Messiah (Anointed One of God) came and died for their sins so that they could have eternal life in heaven. In Luke 23:43 Jesus on the cross told a robber hanging on a cross nearby, "Today thou shalt be with me in Paradise." This was because the man had to go there first while Jesus went to heaven to present his blood as a sacrifice for the sin of all mankind. God the Father had to accept Jesus' sacrificial blood before the former robber could go to heaven. In Matthew 27:51-53 when Jesus arose from the dead, all the saints in Paradise rose up also, and went to heaven. Paradise was empty after their resurrection:

> And, behold, the veil of the temple was rent in twain from the top to the bottom; and the earth did quake, and the rocks rent. And the graves were opened; and many bodies of the saints which slept arose. And came out of the graves after his resurrection, and went into the holy city, and appeared unto many.

Only God in his mercy would create a Paradise for his saints to wait for their cleansing of sin by Jesus' sacrifice.

3. The Pit

The third world in the underworld is called the pit. It is the place where most demons live. Luke 8:26 talks about the demon spirits called Legion. When Jesus commanded them to leave the man, the demons in verse 31 besought Jesus not to command them to go into the pit or abyss.

How do they get out of the pit? They can only come out if a man or woman calls them out. It is not because Satan has not wanted them out, but because no human being has called them out. We see more demons in Africa and Philippines and India because the people there call them out by worshiping idols and directly calling out demons. Matthew 12 shows how they search until they find a place to live. If they do not find a place to live, they have to go back to the pit.

In Revelation 9:1, the saints are gone. The ungodly people that are left are calling the demons out. The falling star mentioned in this verse is Satan. Now he is given the key or permission to release the demons. This chapter shows us that demons have the body of locusts, in the shape of a horse, with the face of a man, long hair like women, teeth like a lions, breastplates, wings, and tails like scorpions. Their number-one goal is to hurt mankind

Sounds like "Star Wars," doesn't it? Don't go to places glorifying creatures that look like demons. If we do, we are out of God's protection. Demons are dangerous and deadly. Believers are commanded to dwell under the shadow of the Almighty (Psalm 91). It is not wise to say we're covered by the blood of Jesus and then go do the things God commanded us not to do. Remember that in the book of Revelation demons had to be commanded not to kill people or do harm to the earth.

4. Tartarus

Tartarus is the Greek word for prison. It is the hellish place where the angels who slept with women in Genesis 6 are housed. 2 Peter 2:4 tells us that God judged the evil angels on the earth who sinned by trying to pollute the seed of the Messiah by sending them into the underworld in chains. But the evil angels that were in the second heaven at that time are still there, as Ephesians 6 reminds us.

And again in Jude 6 and 2 Peter 2:4, God is talking about the angels that did not stay in their habitation in the second heaven but went to earth and in the manner of the people of Sodom and Gomorrah had sex with multiple women on the earth, trying to pollute Adam's seed and stop the coming Messiah. Without a shadow of a doubt, verses 6 and 7 of Jude tell us what the angels did to get their punishment—they went after strange flesh (different from their own) and gave themselves over to fornication (having sex with women). Because of this, God made a special prison for them.

After the resurrection Jesus went into two places. First he went into Paradise (Matthew 27:52) to bring the saints out. Then he went into hell to preach. The theology has been for years that Jesus went into hell to preach to men there to give them a second chance, but that's not in the Bible. 1 Peter 3:19 says he went to hell to preach to "spirits." The Bible never refers to men as spirits. Only angels are called spirits. Also, the Bible says it is appointed unto to man once to die and after that comes the judgment (Hebrews 9:27). Unfortunately, there are no a second chances.

1 Peter 3:19 also makes the Noah connection that Jesus preached to the angels that slept with women that resulted in the flood of Noah. The message Jesus went to preach or proclaim to them was that he'd made it. You see, the evil angels went to prison thinking they had won. But Jesus said, "Hey boys, I'm here," and prepared them for the upcoming judgment.

5. Ghenna

Ghenna means lake of fire. It is empty now but one day will have millions of inhabitants. Matthew 25:41 says the day will come when all the inhabitants of four underworlds will come together there. The original plan was that the lake of fire was to be prepared for the devil, his angels, and demons, but many men and women will go there because of their deep hatred of God. At that time the five worlds will become one. Isaiah 66:24 gives us a startling description of the lake of fire where the pain and torture will be continuous and forever.

Conclusions

To summarize, Lucifer is not almighty. He can be brought down like a lightning bolt falling from the sky. Satan is weaker than we are if we know who we are in Jesus Christ and act on it. Satan also hates us and has no use for us unless we help him propagate his agenda which is total control of heaven and earth. He cheapened his God-given leadership skills by deception and used for evil what he should have been using for good.

He was and is a master of deception. He deceived a third of the angels in heaven and the inhabitants of the earth into believing that he was God. He wants total control of everyone and everything. His true motive is to be God. Be not deceived, though, into believing that he is some cute imp. He is a powerful and dangerous foe who can't be defeated without the help of God. Remember to be like Michael, who didn't fight the devil in his own strength, but said, "The Lord rebukes [or stops] you." Remember to speak the word and let Jesus, the Lord, stop the devil's attack against us.

As mighty as Satan is, keep in mind what the demons said about him in Isaiah 14:10-16, to paraphrase, "He isn't all that great!"

Common Angels

There is not much in the Scriptures on the appearance of archangels, but there are numerous descriptions of common angels of God. Anything to do with the church of Jesus Christ is the job of common angels. Primarily, though, they are involved in assisting and protecting the saved ones or those who have accepted Jesus Christ as their personal Savior. This is confirmed by Hebrews 1:14 which says, "Are they not all ministering spirits, sent forth to minister for them who shall be heirs of salvation?"

Because they are sent to interact with men directly,

they look like men, so much so that they often go unrecognized. This was shown in modern life in the television hit, *Touched by an Angel*, in which all its angels looked like everyday people. This is also seen in Acts 1:10 where Luke tells us "two men stood by them in white apparel." No angel is common, but for lack of a better term we call them common angels.

These common angels are our protectors and keepers on the earth. We will never know how much they've helped us or be able to thank them until we get to heaven. We had better be nice to all men for, as the Bible says in Hebrews 13:2, "Be not forgetful to entertain strangers: for thereby some have entertained angels unaware."

Angel of the Lord

"*Theophanies* refers to the visible appearances of Jesus Christ in other forms prior to his earthly birth. Some passages in the Old Testament tell us that this second person of the Trinity appeared and was called either "the Lord" or "the angel of the Lord." Nowhere is it clearer than in Genesis 18 where three men appear before Abraham. Their leader is clearly identified with the Lord, whereas the other two are merely angels (*Zondervans Pictorial Encyclopedia of the Bible*).

These appearances of God himself as an angel in human form reinforce the idea of the relationship between God and his angels. Nevertheless in almost all the cases where angelic personages appear, they are God's created angelic beings and not God himself.

This God-angel relationship is reinforced by Jewish scholars who call the Angel of the Lord by the name, "Metatron, the angel of countenance," because he witnesses the countenance of God continuously and, therefore, works to extend the program of God for each of us.

These theophany appearances cease in the New

Testament. The obvious theory as to why we don't see the Angel of the Lord in New Testament is that God has given us the fullest revelation of himself—Jesus Christ in the flesh—so he no longer needs to manifest himself in the form of "the Angel of the Lord" in this age of grace. Consequently, the angels who appear in the New Testament or even today are always created spirits and not God in that special angel form that he used in the Old Testament. The appearance of God in the physical form is no longer necessary.

Other Angels: Thrones, Dominions, Powers, Rulers, and Authorities

Some of the Scripture names for angels suggest that they are organized in an orderly fashion. Angels don't "do their own thing" independently of each other. Our evidence for angel organization includes terms used in the New Testament referring to them as "thrones, dominions, powers, rulers, and authorities." This terminology seems to imply different groupings or levels of angelic beings.

Some references seem to be only to evil angelic forces: "Then cometh the end, when he shall have delivered up the kingdom to God, even the Father; when he shall have put down all rule and all authority and power" (1 Corinthians 15:24).

This is also implied in Ephesians 6:12 where Paul says, "For we wrestle not against flesh and blood, but against principalities, against powers, against the rulers of the darkness of this world, against spiritual wickedness in high place." The apostle seems to categorize the five divisions of Satan's army. In his audio-taped series, "Angels: Good, Bad, and Ugly," Tony Evans suggests this breakdown of the five levels:

    1. Our true enemy is not flesh and blood—we are wrestling against low-level evil angels and demons.

    2. "Principalities" in Greek means chief rulers of the

highest rank.

3. "Powers" or "authorities" in Greek means operation under chief rulers and executing their will.

4. "Rulers of the darkness of this world" are men in high authority who are possessed by demonic power or demon ruled.

5. "Wicked spirits in heavenly or high places" are fallen angels.

Other references seem to have only God's good angels in view, as in Ephesians 1:20-21, which tells us God raised Christ

> ... from the dead, and set him at his own right hand in the heavenly places, far above all principality, and power, and might, and dominion, and every name that is named, not only in this world, but also in that which is to come.

Here the Bible seems to be saying that Christ has been exalted and given a name above all, even the angels in the highest position in heaven. Another Scripture example of a "good" angel reference is found in Ephesians 3:10. "His intent was that now, through the church, the manifold wisdom of God should be made known to rulers and authorities in the heavenly realm." God would only give his wisdom to his good angels.

Still other biblical references could easily be both good and evil beings; however, they just may point to the fact that Jesus created all angels and is over all angels.

> For by Christ all things were created; things in heaven and on earth, visible and invisible, whether thrones or powers or rulers or authorities; all things were created by him and for him (Colossians 1:16).
> You have been given fullness in Christ, who is the head over every power and authority (Colossians 2:10).

The good; the bad; the good and bad—confusing isn't it? The point to remember, though, is that in all these passages the vast superiority of Christ in relation to these angelic powers becomes crystal clear.

As you can now see, there are many different types of angels. Angels are real. They are not the product of our imagination but were made by God himself. Whether we see them or not, they are alive and carrying out their God-given purpose. God created a host of angels to help accomplish his work in heaven and on the earth. When we know his Son, Jesus Christ, we can have confidence that one of these mighty and varied creatures will watch over us and assist us because we belong to God.

Test the angels: Knowing the difference between good and evil angels

As we have already seen, angels are vital beings in God's kingdom. They are God's ministering servants. The Bible tells us that they worship before his throne in heaven, having direct access to his presence. They are also God's messengers. In addition, angels are God's warriors, doing battle against the armies of Satan. And at God's command, they watch over us and protect us.

My quarrel here is not with angels—I wouldn't dare quarrel with angels!—but with demons who claim to be angels and are not, and with angels who claim to speak for God, but who in reality lost that right countless years ago!

So don't quarrel or wonder. The Bible tells us to "test the spirits" in order to be certain that they are of God. That's why I'm including this section in this study of angels—because it's important to be able to discern whether or not an angel comes from God or from the devil. The Scriptures tell us that Satan can disguise himself as an "angel of light" (2 Corinthians 11:14). The Bible also tells us that at the end of this age even the very elect of God will be deceived (Matthew 24:24). So that we won't be fooled, let's consider a few tests.

If you ever encounter anyone who says he is an angel of God or someone who says they have a message from God and you want to know if they truly are of God or of the devil, the apostle John tells us how we can test their spirit. Evil angels, demons, and demon influenced or possessed people can't handle the presence of Christ and always are repelled from his presence (they can't stand being reminded of their final outcome). So we test the spirit behind them by testing their response to Jesus Christ. Look at 1 John 4:1-6 for a description of the test:

> Beloved, believe not every spirit, but try the spirits whether they are of God, because many false prophets are gone out into the world. Hereby know ye the Spirit of God: Every spirit that confesseth that Jesus Christ is come in the flesh is of God: And every spirit that confesseth not that Jesus Christ is come in the flesh is not of God. This is that spirit of antichrist, whereof ye have heard that it should come; and even now already is it in the world.
>
> Ye are of God, little children, and have overcome them: because greater is he that is in you, than he that is in the world. They are of the world: therefore speak they of the world, and the world heareth them. We are of God: he that knoweth God heareth us; he that is not of God heareth not us. Hereby know we the spirit of truth, and the spirit of error.

Matthew Henry's *Concise Commentary of the Scripture* presents the meat of what this verse means:

> The sum of revealed religion is in the doctrine concerning Christ, his person, and office. The false teachers spoke of the world according to

44

its maxims and tastes, so as not to offend carnal men. The world approved them, they made rapid progress, and had many followers such as themselves; the world will love its own, and its own will love it.

The true doctrine as to the Savior's person [in the flesh] as leading men from the world to God, is a mark of the spirit of truth in opposition to the spirit of error. The more pure and holy any doctrine is, the more likely to be of God; nor can we by any other rules try the spirits whether they are of God or not. And what wonder is it that people of a worldly spirit should cleave to those who are like themselves, and suit their schemes and discourses to their corrupt taste?

Godly angels or teachers of the Bible will always present Jesus Christ the man, who is the way to God. Their teaching will be a pure and holy doctrine always in line with the Bible and not some new revelation unsubstantiated by Scripture.

Yes, God's angels always act and speak in line with the Holy Scriptures, but are elusive in nature. Most of the time they stay in the background, silent and invisible. Other times we may encounter them and not even know that we were in their presence. That's why the book of Hebrews says, "Do not forget to entertain strangers, for by so doing some people have entertained angels without knowing it" (13:2). This is also the reason we have to test whose spirit is behind their message right then and there, because the next minute they might be gone and we never see them again. So let's look a little closer at the differences between God's angels and Satan's angels.

God's angels:
·   Are God's warriors and messengers, and as

such, they will never tell you anything that is contrary to his word as contained in the Bible
· Are never willing to accept the praise or worship of human beings
· Always seek to bring glory to God and his Son, Jesus Christ
· Rejoice whenever a sinner comes into God's kingdom through the only means possible— faith in Christ
· Understand that we are all powerless apart from God
· Are ministering spirits who walk alongside the faithful, ministering to and encouraging those who strive to live for God
· Come to us to lead us to God.

Satan's angels:
· Are his warriors and his messengers, and as such they often claim to be bringing "new and better truths" to replace or update what is contained in the Bible
· Readily accept and even invite human praise and worship
· Deny or downplay Christ's divinity
· Say that there are many paths to peace with God
· Tell us that we have the power within us to be- come like God
· Are anxious to take control
· Come to us to lead us away from God

Another reason we need this test is because an evil doctrine may not always look perverted; in fact, it may look downright good. 2 Corinthians 11:13-15 tells us that not all men who call themselves apostles of Jesus Christ are. It goes on to say that if even Satan can disguise himself as an "angel of light," why should we be surprised if his ministers do also. We should look at what the potential fruit or outcome in our lives would be. Would an outcome of this doctrine reflect the Spirit of God or the devil? In essence, we have to read and know the holy Scripture for ourselves or a doctrine of the devil may ride into our lives.

One final note. When people of the Bible encountered angels, they were always struck with terror and fear. When practitioners of the occult meet their angels, they are often filled with warm fuzzies. What's the mix-up?

CHAPTER THREE

Characteristics of God's Angels

I heard my grandma say one time, "God took that little girl because he wanted another angel in heaven." That may sound good, but it is not true. As we have seen in our discussion on the origins of angels, human beings are not angels, and when they die and go to heaven, they will not turn into angels. Angels are angels and humans are humans. The scientific world will tell you that there are certain key characteristics that make humans human, and so it is with angels.

The following story addresses two of the angelic characteristics; their function of guardianship, and their form—wings. In this story told by Lloyd Glenn on Catholic Online in 1994, a three-year-old boy's guardian angel rescues him from a catastrophic injury, and then Jesus, the Light, gives him the charge and the ability to tell the world about "the birdies." The boy's father shares the story.

The "Birdies"

On July 22nd I was enroute to Washington, DC for a business trip. It was all so very ordinary, until we landed in Denver for a plane change. As I collected my belongings from the overhead bin, an announcement was made for Mr. Lloyd Glenn to see the United Airlines customer service representative immediately. I thought nothing of it until I reached the door to leave the plane and I heard a gentleman asking every male if they were Mr. Glenn. At this point I knew something was wrong and my heart sank.

When I got off the plane, a solemn-faced young man came toward me and said, "Mr. Glenn, there is an emergency at your home. I do not know what the emergency is, or who is involved, but I will take you to the phone so you can call the hospital." My heart was now pounding, but the will to be calm took over. Woodenly, I followed this stranger to the distant telephone where I called the number that he gave me for the Mission Hospital.

My call was put through to the trauma center where I learned that my three-year-old son had been trapped underneath the automatic garage door for several minutes and that, when my wife had found him, he was dead. CPR had been performed by a neighbor, who is a doctor, and the paramedics had continued the treatment as Brian was transported to the hospital. By the time of my call, Brian was revived, and they believed he would live, but they did not know how much damage had been done to his brain, nor to his heart.

They explained that the door had completely closed on his little sternum right over his heart. He had been severely crushed. After speaking with the medical staff, my wife sounded worried but not hysterical, and I took comfort in her calmness. The return flight seemed to last forever, but finally I arrived at the hospital six hours after the garage door had come down. When I walked into the intensive care unit, nothing could have prepared me to see my little son lying so still on a great big bed with tubes and monitors everywhere. He was also on a respirator.

I glanced at my wife who stood and tried to give me a

reassuring smile. It all seemed like a terrible dream. I was filled in with the details and given a guarded prognosis. Brian was going to live, and the preliminary tests indicated that his heart was okay, two miracles in and of themselves. Only time would tell if his brain sustained any damage.

Throughout the seemingly endless hours, my wife was calm. She felt that Brian would eventually be all right. I hung on to her words and faith like a lifeline. All that night and the next day Brian remained unconscious. It seemed like forever since I had left for my business trip the day before. Finally at two o'clock that afternoon, our son regained consciousness and sat up, uttering the most beautiful words I have ever heard: "Daddy, hold me," and he reached for me with his little arms.

By the next day he was pronounced as having no neurological or physical deficits, and the story of his miraculous survival spread throughout the hospital. One cannot imagine our gratitude and joy. As we took Brian home, we felt a unique reverence for the life and love of our heavenly Father that comes to those who brush death so closely. In the days that followed there was a special spirit about our home. Our two older children were much closer to their little brother. My wife and I were much closer to each other, and all of us were very close as a whole family. Life took on a less stressful pace. Perspective seemed to be more focused, and balance much easier to gain and maintain. We felt deeply blessed. Our gratitude was truly profound.

Almost a month later to the day of the accident, Brian awoke from his afternoon nap and said, "Sit down, Mommy. I have something to tell you." At this time in his life, Brian usually spoke in small phrases, so for him to say a large sentence surprised my wife. She sat down with him on his bed, and he began his remarkable story.

"Do you remember when I got stuck under the garage

door? Well, it was so heavy and it hurt really bad. I called to you, but you couldn't hear me. I started to cry, but then it hurt too bad. And then the 'birdies' came."

"The 'birdies'?" my wife asked, puzzled.

"Yes," he replied. "The 'birdies' made a whooshing sound and flew into the garage. They took care of me."

"They did?"

"Yes," he said. "One of the 'birdies' came and got you. She came to tell you I got stuck under the door."

A sweet reverent feeling filled the room. The spirit was so strong and yet lighter than air. My wife realized that a three-year-old had no concept of death and spirits, so he was referring to the angels who came to him from beyond as "birdies" because they were up in the air like birds that fly. "What did the birdies look like?" she asked.

Brian answered, "They were so beautiful. They were dressed in white, all white. Some of them had green and white. But some of them had on just white."

"Did they say anything?"

"Yes," he answered. "They told me that the baby would be all right."

"The baby?" my wife asked, confused.

And Brian answered, "The baby laying on the garage floor."

He went on, "You came out and opened the garage door and ran to the baby. You told the baby to stay and not to leave."

My wife nearly collapsed upon hearing this, for she had indeed gone and knelt beside Brian's body and seeing his crushed chest and unrecognizable features, knowing that he was already dead, she had looked up and whispered, "Don't leave us, Brian. Please stay if you can." As she listened to Brian telling her the words that she had indeed spoken, she realized that the spirit had left his body and was looking down from above on this little lifeless form. "Then what happened?" she asked.

"We went on a trip," he said, "far, far away." He grew agitated trying to say the things he didn't seem to have the words for. My wife tried to calm and comfort him, and let him know it would be O.K. He struggled with wanting to tell something that obviously was very important to him, but finding the words was difficult.

"We flew so fast up in the air. They're so pretty, Mommy," he added. "And there are lots and lots of 'birdies.'" My wife was stunned. Into her mind the sweet, comforting spirit enveloped her more soundly, but with an urgency she had never before known.

Brian went on to tell her that the birdies had told him that he had to come back and tell everyone about the birdies. He said they brought him back to the house and that a big fire truck and an ambulance were there. A man was bringing the baby out on a white bed and he tried to tell the man the baby would be okay, but the man couldn't hear him. He said that the birdies had told him that he had to go with the ambulance but that they would be near him. He said, they were so pretty and so peaceful that he didn't want to come back.

And then the bright light came. He said that the light was so bright and so warm, and he loved the bright light so much. Someone was in the bright light and put their arms around him and told him, "I love you, but you have to go back. You have to play baseball, and tell everyone about the birdies." Then the person in the bright light kissed him and waved goodbye. Then whoosh, the big sound came, and they went into the clouds.

The story went on for an hour. He taught us that "birdies" were always with us, but that we don't see them because we look with our eyes, and we don't hear them because we listen with our ears. But they are always there. You can only see them in here (he put his hand over his heart). They whisper the things to help us to do what is right because they love us so much.

Three-year-old Brian continued, stating, "I have a plan, Mommy. You have a plan. Daddy has a plan. Everyone has a plan. We must all live our plan and keep our promises. The 'birdies' help us to do that 'cause they love us so much." In the weeks that followed he often came to us and told all or part of it again and again. Always the story remained the same. The details were never changed or out of order. A few times he added further bits of information and clarified the message he had already delivered. It never ceased to amaze us how he could tell such detail and speak beyond his ability when he spoke of his "birdies." Everywhere he went, he told strangers about the birdies. Surprisingly, no one ever looked at him strangely when he did this. Rather, they always get a softened look on their face and smiled. Needless to say, we have not been the same ever since that day, and I pray we never will be.

We can learn much from three-year-old Brian. Excuse me, but I can't get off the fact that this is a three-year-old talking. Just as when, after Jesus' crucifixion, the disciples were preaching and the religious leaders of the day marveled at the way they spoke with such eloquence and wisdom, because they were simple fishermen. Then they remembered that they had been with Jesus. So it is with Brian.

As a registered nurse, I know that it would have been impossible for a child with three-year-old cognitive and verbal skills to relate the information on the "birdies" with such detail, clarity, and complete sentence structure. The angels may have been in the miracle, but also remember he had been with the Light—Jesus.

It is the light of Jesus their Creator that the angels' characteristics reflect. So let's learn more about the characteristics of angels from what the Bible says about them. In general, they are spirit beings created by God to serve God in a specific role. Both good and evil angels have some of these characteristics, but for the evil angels who chose to side with Satan during his mutinous attempt, godly traits went out the window. Like humans, angels have specific God-given jobs and gifts, but certain characteristics of these godly angels are common to all. We will discuss a few.

Angels are persons

Angels are personal beings or have a personhood. In order to be a person, a being must have three things: emotion, will, and intellect. Angels have all three. We will discuss their will and intellect or wisdom in the next two sections. Regarding their emotions, 1 Peter 1:12 shows that angels have the emotion of desire in that they longed to know more about the experience of salvation (see the "Angels Are Curious" section just ahead). Angels also get excited and want to party, as described in Luke 15:10 when Jesus says the angels rejoice when one person gets saved. Why are they so excited? One more victory for God in the angelic battle over the souls of men.

Angels have a will

A description of an angel that exerted his will above all—even God—is found in the Isaiah 14:12-15 discussion on the fall of Lucifer. Lucifer was an archangel who decided or willed to become like God and convinced one-third of heaven's angels to follow him. This is the greatest example of an angel exerting his will in a situation. Angels have a will—they can choose to do things. That's why Satan fell. He made a conscious choice not to obey God. On the other hand, God's angels chose to serve and be obedient to him.

Angels are wise

2 Samuel 14:20 tells us outright that angels are wise,

"My lord is wise according to the wisdom of an angel of God." Angels are wise because they are inspired by the Holy Spirit. Nothing is hidden from them about earthly matters. They know everything happening in the earth—every problem, every political situation.

Even though angels are exceedingly wise and are far more knowledgeable than humans, they don't know everything. Jesus, when talking about his return, said, "But about that day and hour no one knows, neither the angels of heaven, nor the Son, but only the Father" (Matthew 24:36). They are not like God who knows every-thing. They do, however, know things about us we don't even know about ourselves. Since they help and guide us, this knowledge will always be used for good, not evil purposes. At a time when few people can be trusted, it's nice to know the angels won't reveal our deepest secrets. Instead, they use what they know only for our good.

Angels are spirit beings
They have no physical bodies. The Bible describes them as we have already seen in Hebrews 1:14, "Are they not all ministering spirits sent to minister to [or serve] the heirs of salvation?" A.W. Tozer describes a spirit being this way:

> Existence on a level above matter; it means life subsisting in another mode. A spirit is substance that has no weight, no dimension, no size nor extension in space. These quali-ties belong to matter and can have no appli-cation to spirit. Yet a spirit has true being and is objectively real. (*The Pursuit of God*, 1948).

Angels meet this description of a spirit. They are not made up of physical matter but of spiritual matter. They have no flesh and bones, no breath or gills, but appar-ently they do eat, because Psalm 78:25 tells us that there is a "bread of angels." However, it is their spiritual nature and holiness that allows them to go back and forth before the throne of God, bringing us help and answered prayers. Angels have material bodies in comparison to God, because God exists on a far higher spiritual level than they, and because they are limited in that they can't be in two places at the same time. God, on the other hand, can be everywhere at the same time, or you could say he is omnipresent. If a spirit being can be summoned at will, then it is not an angel of God:

> So Saul disguised himself . . . and came to the [medium at Endor] by night. And he said, "Consult a spirit for me, and bring up for me the one whom I name to you . . ." Then the woman said, "Whom shall I bring up for you?" (1 Samuel 28:8-11, NRSV).

Even though angels are invisible spirit beings, they do become visible at times to carry out God's sovereign commands. Sometimes when God wants to accomplish something, he will direct an invisible angel to become visible in the life of a believer in order to accomplish some divinely ordained timetable for doing God's will. For example, in Genesis 18 they looked like men in order to tell Sarah she would have a baby when she was 90, and then Abraham entertained them. Angels were used as a vehicle of God for addressing a supernatural miracle about to happen in their life.

Angels are immortal

Billy Graham in his book *Angels, God's Secret Agents* wrote,

> The Scriptures do not tell us what elements make up angels . . . The Bible seems to indicate that angels do not age and never says that one was sick. Except for those who fell with Lucifer, the ravages of sin that have brought destruction, sickness, and chaos to

our earth have not affected them. The holy angels will never die.

He feels they are immortal and walk the paths of eternity. Jesus confirms this when he tells us in Luke 20:36, "Those who are raised to eternity, can no longer die, for they are like angels." It's comforting to know that we will share heaven with God's holy angels. I think all Christians everywhere look forward to that day when we no longer experience the aches and pains of life and of growing old.

Angels are powerful

Angels have remarkable God-given power over the natural world. "Peter and the angel came before the iron gate leading into the city. It opened for them of its own accord" (Acts 12:10). This is not the act of some wimpy, baby-faced being, but one of power.

Angels are powerful warriors:

> Then [Gabriel] said, "Now I must return to fight against the prince of Persia, and when I am through with him, the prince of Greece will come . . . There is no one with me who contends against these princes except Michael, your prince" (Daniel 10:20-21).

Revelation 18:1 gives us another view of angelic power, showing how they excel in strength. "And after these things I saw another angel come down from heaven, having great power; and the earth was lightened with his glory." Imagine, an angel so powerful that the whole earth is lit up with the glory of God.

Again in Isaiah 37:36 we see the power of one angel:

> Then the angel of the LORD went out and put to death a hundred and eighty-five thousand men in the Assyrian camp. When the people got up the next morning, there were all the dead bodies!

I also believe that an angel's sword symbolizes the power of God that backs up an angel's ministry. "David looked up and saw the angel of the Lord standing between earth and heaven, and in his hand a drawn sword stretched out over Jerusalem" (1 Chronicles 21:16).

Evil angels are powerful and use their God-given power against him. Ephesians 6 mentions some of them, describing them as powers, principalities, and rulers of the darkness of this world, as we saw earlier.

Yes, angels are powerful beings, as we see when in Luke 24:2-5 they whisked away a stone the size of a door as if it were paper; or when angels controlled nature in Revelation 7:1 as they held back the winds of the earth; or when in Revelation 8:12 they sounded a horn and the moon and one-third of the stars were smitten; or in Revelation 16:8 when they poured the bowl of wrath out on the sun, causing it to scorch people. In addition, 2 Thessalonians 1:7 informs us that when Jesus returns, it will be with his most powerful angels.

Angels are powerful, indeed, but, as powerful as they are, they are not all-powerful like God. They have no force or power of their own. They use the power or energy God has given them. Even a child knows that the creator is always greater than the created.

Angels have personality plus and are perfect communicators

God's angels always make their message clear, because they only speak the word of the Lord. Their personality, however, reflects their function. Their function is to worship and serve God and have his power flowing through them to protect and help the people on the earth who are heirs of salvation. So it would be natural to assume that they would have sound, action-oriented personalities with great wisdom.

It is this sound, action-oriented communication that

helps them to clarify God's will for your life. They help you to plan and succeed in life. When you don't know what to do, the angels will come and lead you in the right direction. In Acts 5:19-20 an angel opened the door and told Peter to go stand in the temple and speak to the people. Even though angels are a great help, never look directly to angels for the help.

Colossians 2:18 says that we must not pray to or worship angels. We can elicit their help by praying to the Lord, and he will send his angel to direct our way. Psalm 103:20 provides proof of this. Describing God's angels, this text says they "excel in strength and do his commandments, harkening to the voice of his word."

Which is another way to get them to help you by speaking the word of God, Scripture from the Bible, over your situation. Remember, they harken to the voice of God's words. So your voice speaking God's word over your situation will invoke the angels into action for your behalf. In other words, angels respond or pay attention to the voice of the Lord or God's word—not to our panicky prayers. Our job is to pray to God and speak his word over our situations in life, and it is God's part to send his angels to help us. God's angels will always point you to God.

Although angels perfectly communicate with men on the earth, they have their own language. "If I speak in tongues of mortals and angels, but do not have love, I am a noisy gong or a clanging cymbal" (1 Corinthians 13:1, NRSV).

Nothing exceeds the exquisite courtesy of angels. "And [Gabriel] came to [Mary] and said, 'Greetings, favored one. The Lord is with you'" (Luke 1:28, NASB). A southern gentleman has nothing on an angel of the Lord.

Another beautiful aspect of godly angelic communication when dealing with mankind is that they invite, not compel. They never interfere with our free choice. "An angel of the Lord appeared to him in a dream and said, Joseph, son of David, do not be afraid to take Mary as your wife. For the child conceived in her is from the Holy Spirit" (Matthew 1:20). When Joseph awoke, he felt an assurance that all would be well and went ahead and took Mary as his wife.

Also, God not only sends special angels into our lives, but sometimes he even sends them back again if we forget to take notes the first time!

> Then Manoah entreated the Lord and said, O Lord, I pray let the man of God whom you sent come to me again and teach us. God listened to Manoah, and the angel of God came again (Judges 13:8, NRSV).

The angel explained the thing again until he was sure Manoah understood.

Here are some examples of angel talk in the Bible. I think they reflect their powerful intellect and communication skills.

· Look with your eyes and hear with your ears and pay attention to everything I am going to show you, for that is why you have been brought here (Ezekiel 40:4).

· I have now come to give you insight and understanding (Daniel 9:22).

· I have come to explain to you what will happen to your people in the future, for the vision concerns a time yet to come (Daniel 10:14).

· I will tell you what is written in the Book of Truth (Daniel 10:21).

· There will be a time of distress such as has not

happened from the beginning of nations until then . . . Multitudes who sleep in the dust of the earth will awake, some to everlasting life, others to shame and everlasting contempt (Daniel 12:1-2).

· We have gone throughout the earth and found the whole world at rest and in peace (Zechariah 1:11).

· Your wife . . . will bear you a son . . . He will go on before the Lord . . . to turn the hearts of the fathers to their children and the disobedient to the wisdom of the righteous to make ready a people prepared for the Lord (Luke 1:13-17).

· I am Gabriel. I stand in the presence of God, and I have been sent to speak to you and to tell you this good news. And now you will be silent and not able to speak (Luke 1:19).

· Do not be afraid. I bring you good news of great joy that will be for all the people (Luke 2:10).

· Why do you look for the living among the dead? He is not here, he has risen! (Luke 24:5-6).

· There will be no more delay . . . the mystery of God will be accomplished (Revelation 10:6-7).

· The kingdom of the world has become the kingdom of our Lord and his Christ, and he will reign forever and ever (Revelation 11:15).

As you can see, these angels speak with style and class, much like God speaks. Well, no wonder. When you're around speaking perfection in heaven, it just has to rub off on you. They speak and act with such eloquence while carrying out the Lord's will. Let's hope we all speak like God when we get to heaven also.

Angels are curious

In particular, angels are curious about our salvation. The apostle Peter, speaking about salvation, says in 1 Peter 1:12, "Even angels long to look into these things." What does Peter mean? Surely the angels know the details of our salvation; since they were there when the first person was converted. Angels can't understand this great mercy afforded to us because they have never sinned.

Angels do have a head knowledge of our salvation, but they haven't felt, feasted on it, or experienced it. They are curious about what it feels like to be forgiven of sins and to be born again. God's angels can't understand this great mercy given to us because they have never sinned.

They long to look into these things because they know that personal experience is far better than mental understanding. The Greek word translated "to look into" is a term that pictures someone "stooping over to look." This is not a quick glance, but a calculated, close-up analysis, a deliberate gaze, a studied observation. They already know about salvation; they long instead to stoop over and experience it. They are curious about these things and want to study, examine, and analyze to understand how we can endure such things and continue in the hope and peace only God can give.

This salvation or born again experience that the angels are curious about can be summarized like this. People who make a willful choice to accept salvation through the blood Jesus shed on the cross as a substitution before God for payment for all their sins—past, present, and future—are spiritually sprinkled with Jesus' blood and can stand clean and sinless before God. These people can have the spiritual, heartfelt knowledge that they will have everlasting life with God in heaven. Angels will never know this cleansing that's available only to men. They will never know the freshness of being born again. This new birth comes our way through God's great mercy (1 Peter 1:3). God's angels have never needed his mercy because they've never sinned. It feels kind of good to be one up on the angels, doesn't it. It feels good to be forgiven. Angels can only long to experience this—but we already have.

Angels are often unrecognizable

I wonder how many times angels have come in and out of our lives and we never recognized who they were.

> Peter went out and followed the angel; he did not realize that what was happening with the angel's help was real; he thought he was seeing a vision. (Acts 12:9).

> Now [Balaam] was riding his donkey and his two servants were with him. The donkey saw the angel of the Lord standing in the road, with a drawn sword in his hand; so the donkey turned off the road and went into the field. Balaam beat her to get her back on the road. (Numbers 22:22-23, NRSV).

Balaam did not see the angel.

Angels Modus Operandum

A Modus Operandum (MO) can be defined as a method of operating or a way a person habitually does things. Many people have been aided by the doings of these mysterious angelic strangers. The angels' primary MO is that they appear, seemingly out of nowhere, in moments of distress, during a disaster, after an accident, or whenever we find ourselves in a hopeless situation, and then suddenly disappear when the task is completed.

Sandra Ridge of Fostoria, Ohio, offers us an example:

"I was having dinner with my family at a fast-food restaurant when my husband began choking. A piece of food had lodged in his throat. His face was beet red. I didn't know what to do and neither did the other diners. We were helpless as my husband was choking to death. Suddenly the door opened and a strong looking middle-aged woman walked past the cashiers and other patrons right to our table. She put her arms around Greg, placing a fist just below his rib cage and pushed with a quick upward thrust of her other hand. Out popped the piece of food. His face returned to its normal color as he caught his breath. I held him tightly, thanking the Lord for the woman who served him. I looked around to thank her but she was gone. The cashiers said she wasn't a customer; she hadn't ordered food at all. As quickly as she appeared, she vanished—as though she was an angel on assignment to rescue Greg. It was a meal I'll never forget."

Also, a part of a person's MO is their presentation or how they look. Billy Graham in his book on angels does an excellent job of describing their physical attributes:

> God is forever imaginative, colorful, and glorious in what he designs. Some of the descriptions of angels, including the one of Lucifer in Ezekiel 28, indicate that they are exotic to the human eye and mind. Apparently angels have a beauty and variety that surpass anything known to men.

The Bible description of angels is indeed exotic, as seen in Ezekiel 1:6-9, Isaiah 6:1-4, and in the book of Revelation. According to biblical descriptions, they can either look just like us or they can appear like nothing on earth, such as the one found in Ezekiel 1:6-9:

Each had four faces, and each of them had

four wings. Their legs were straight, and the soles of their feet were like the sole of a calf's foot, and they sparkled like burnish bronze. Under their wings on their four sides, they had human hands.

Even though angels may look exotic in heaven, they present themselves on earth in such a way that the person needing help will be open to them. *Angels on the Earth* magazine presented a story about an angel who came in the form of a dog. The lady the angel was sent to rescue was wary of human strangers but loved dogs. In the end, the angel-dog led the lady to safety and then disappeared when it saw she was safe.

While one angel appeared to this lady in the form of a dog, they most often appear in the form of human beings to protect, guide, and save us when situations are beyond our control. This is the most common manifestation of angels. Angels can present in the form of a male or female, and any race or nationality.

Even though they may appear as male or female, the Bible teaches that angels are sexless. Jesus said that in heaven men neither marry, nor are given in marriage, but are as angels of God in heaven (Matthew 22:30). This may indicate that angels enjoy relationships that are far more thrilling and exciting than anything humans have ever known.

Most often, though, they usually appear as a clean-cut, well-dressed male. They are polite and knowledgeable about the crisis, and quickly take charge. They speak softly and sparingly. They can eat real food (Genesis 18:8), and they seem as human as the rest of us. When the problem they are addressing is solved, they vanish. In fact, their appearance just in the nick of time and disappearance when thanks is about to be given, is typical of God's angels. Here's my experience.

Roller blade angel

One day while I was taking my morning walk in
Trinity Park in Fort Worth, Texas, I saw a group of young
men in their twenties a little ways up the walking path.
Because the Trinity Park walking path has a few
stretches where you can see almost a mile in front and
behind you, I could see them looking at me. I became
troubled, but then I thought, *Surely they won't try anything funny in broad daylight.* But I would soon find out I
was wrong.

I hurried past them, trying to ignore their cat-calls
and whistling. Suddenly something said, *Look back.* I
looked back and three of the men were starting to follow
me in a slow jog.

Panicking, I prayed, "Jesus, help me!" I looked up
and a tall, slender young man dressed in a T-shirt and
shorts on roller blades was coming toward me. He smiled
and said, "Good morning." It startled me because I could
have sworn that no one was there a minute ago. I tripped
and fell. The man on the roller blades stopped and helped
me up. As I looked up and into his kind eyes, I noticed he
had those and-Jesus-looked-at-them eyes that see
straight through you. Remembering the group of men
that were following me, I looked back to see if they were
still there. They were running fast in the opposite direction as if they had seen something terrible. *What's going
on? I thought.* I turned back to thank the young man for
helping me up and he was gone. I could see at least a half
a mile of the walking path in front of me, and there was
no sign of him. *Where did he go?* Then I thought of my
prayer for help. An angel. I knew angels came in many
forms, but I never expected to see one on roller blades!

Angels do appear in many forms. We all see angels. If
we never recognize them, it's because they come in ways
we don't expect. So we should be hospitable to strangers,

because we may unknowingly be in the presence of angels.

Another part of the angels' MO is that they bring answers to our prayers, and they will even do great battle with evil forces of hell to get the answer to us. An example of this is found in Daniel 10, where a dazzling angel fought the Prince of Persia for twenty-one days to get the answer to Daniel's prayer to him. Another example of this is found in Acts 10:3-5, where Cornelius prayed for help in becoming a follower of Jesus Christ. An angel told him to go get Peter. Cornelius obeyed the angel, sent and got Peter, and was converted.

Lastly, one more thing on the subject. When angels appear, people often comment about the bright light that surrounds them. They say that there is a glow or radiance associated with the appearance of God's angels. This is because the glory of God is on them, as in Daniel 10:5-6. When the angel of the Lord showed up, the brightness was more than Daniel's eyes could handle. Also in Acts 12:7 when the angel appeared, a light was shining about him. Again, angels of the Lord have great light associated with them because the glory of the Lord is on them. We have seen that Hebrews 1:7 calls them flames of fire, perhaps because of their brilliance. On resurrection morning, Matthew tells us, "An angel of the Lord, descended from heaven . . . His appearance was like lightning and his clothing white as snow" (28:3).

Because God's light and glory are upon his angels, they are often mistaken for God. If it seems that angels rarely appear, it's because we all too often mistake the medium for the Message. "Then I fell down at [the angel's] feet to worship him, but he said to me, 'You must not do that! I am a fellow servant with you and your comrades who hold the testimony of Jesus. Worship God!'" (Revelation 19:10). This is what got Lucifer in trouble. He wanted to be mistaken for the Message and receive all the glory and worship for himself.

Angels have halos

It is because of this angelic brightness that the halo became a symbol of these heavenly beings in the fourth century. It signified divine radiance from their nearness to God. The halo, often worn by angels, was used to signify a supernatural force and superior intellect and advanced spiritual development. The halo was also used by master artists of old to identify who was an angel and who was human.

In the television program, *Touched by an Angel*, the light surrounding the angels is so bright it is startling, but it is completely scriptural. The program always shows the person's first reaction to the angels as fear and awe, and, just like in the Bible, the angels of *Touched by an Angel* always have to tell the people to fear not. Angels need to tell us not to be afraid, because they shine as if they just came from the very throne room of Almighty God. "Then the woman came and told her husband, 'A man of God came to me, and his appearance was like that of an angel, most awe-inspiring'" (Judges 13:6, NRSV).

Angels are innumerable

How many angels are there? It's a question that's been pondered since before the Bible was written. In Daniel 7:10, the prophet had a vision of ten thousand times ten thousand—or one hundred million. Modern angel experts say that there are as many angels in the universe as are necessary for each child of God to have one, plus a few to spare. We never have to worry about there not being enough angels to go around. As many as we need—that's how many are available to help us.

Although the Bible does not give an exact count of angels, there is evidence that there are multitudes of them. Hebrews 12:22 gives a graphic picture of their large numbers, "Thousands upon thousands of angels in joyful assembly." Jesus himself gives us a picture also of massive numbers of angels. Right after the soldiers came to arrest him and he was trying to stop his disciples from fighting, he said, "Do you think I cannot call on my Father, and he will at once put at my disposal more than twelve legions of angels?" (Matthew 26:53). Now remember a legion can be anywhere between three and six thousand men, more than enough to take care of a few earthly soldiers. In Psalm 68:17, David, speaking of angelic warriors, said, "The chariots of God are tens of thousands and thousands of thousands."

One last verse. The apostle John in Revelation 5:11 "looked and heard the voice of many angels, numbering thousands upon thousands, and ten thousands time ten thousand. They encircled the throne."

All this mentioning of numbers in the Bible was probably an attempt by these men to quantify the massive hosts of angels they saw. Imagine yourself in a filled-to-capacity football stadium. Would you be able to count the exact number of people there? Probably not, and neither were they able to. Let's just say there are too many to count.

Angels have battles

Angels have struggles or battles in their lives, but these are usually struggles related to God and his enemy Satan. Archangel Gabriel, speaking to Daniel, said he was delayed by a battle with a demonic ruler, and that Michael, an archangel had to come to help him to get through to bring an answer to Daniel's prayer (Daniel 10:13). God is the only one with all power, as Gabriel concludes in Luke 1:37, "Nothing is impossible with God."

Angels have wings

That angels have wings is not just a figment of the imagination of the artists of old. Angels really do have wings. This is verified in many books of the Bible, most dramatically in the Isaiah 6 description of the seraphim, the Ezekiel 1 description of the cherubim, and the Revelation 4 description of the living creatures.

These wings are not just useless accessories. Angels use their wings to fly. Daniel 9:21 describes how Gabriel flew in to give Daniel the answer to his prayer, and in Revelation 14:6 John describes an angel flying in midair. And what about Brian's "birdies"?

Angels fly at the speed of light, because they are servants of the Light. "He rode on a cherub and flew. He came swiftly upon the wings of the wind" (Psalm 18:10).

Angels are agents of wrath

As we know, God is a good God, but he is also a just, righteous, and holy God. What this means is that sin must be accounted for. Someone must pay for unforgiven sin. Sin is forgiven in the Old Testament by the sacrificing of animals, and in the New Testament by a person choosing to accept Jesus the Christ's substitutionary death on the cross for their sins. This is where God's wrath comes in.

Although God wants to forgive all men through his Son's death on the cross, if a person chooses not to accept this way to forgiveness, God will deal with the sin, and this is done many times through his angels. The following are just a few examples of how angels are used as warriors of wrath:

> · Genesis 3:24 - Angels standing guard at the entrance of the Garden of Eden with a flaming sword flashing back and forth. They are armed soldiers sent by God to prevent Adam and Eve from returning to the Garden of Eden and eating the fruit of the tree of life.

> · 2 Samuel 24:15-17 and 1 Chronicles 21:14-17 - The angel with the sword in his hand was holding the

power of the plague that had already killed seventy thousand people and was poised to strike the city of Jerusalem when King David confessed in agony, "I am the one who sinned." And another voice clapped like thunder saying, "Enough!" And the angel put the sword back into its sheath.

· 2 Kings 19:35; 2 Chronicles 32:21; Isaiah 37:36 - The Assyrians' massive army was camped outside of Jerusalem, preparing to attack. When the night fell, the angel of the Lord appeared, and his work was done in a moment. The next morning the Jews found 185,000 dead Assyrians.

· In Acts 12:21-23 - When King Herod accepts the people's praise, "This is the voice of a god, not a man," the angel of the Lord suddenly stands behind the throne and touches the king's body, and Herod falls to the floor with worms devouring him from the inside out.

· Revelation 8 - Here, seven angels release seven golden bowls filled with the wrath of God, killing a third of mankind.

As you can see, angels are awesome warriors and agents of God's wrath and power. But as great as they are, according to Hebrews 1:3, Jesus is better than the angels. Although angels are great and awesome, look to Jesus.

CHAPTER FOUR

The Role of Angels With God

The role of angels with God is simple but multifaceted in nature. Listed below is a grocery list of the main roles of angels with God. It certainly is not all-inclusive. We won't know all their jobs until we get to heaven. Then we will get to see them work with God firsthand.

To proclaim, promote, and uplift God

If we could speak with tongues of angels, our first word would always be *God*. "And one seraph called to another and said, Holy, holy, holy is the Lord of Hosts" (Isaiah 6:3).

To speak the will of God

Angels only speak to us with the voice or words of the God who sent them. So if you come across someone claiming to be an angel of God and he says something that goes against what the Bible says, then he is a messenger not of God and is most likely one sent by the enemy of God, the devil. "I am going to send an angel in front of you to guard you on the way . . . Be attentive to him and listen to his voice for my name is in him" (Exodus 23:20-21).

To do the will of God

Angels are not free agents who do as they please.

Like Jesus, they come to do the will of the One who sent them. "Bless the Lord, O you his angels, you mighty ones who do his bidding, obedient to his spoken word. Bless the Lord, all his hosts, his ministering spirits who do his will" (Psalm 103:20-21). For every angel whose ministry is on earth, a million angels praise God in heaven. "A thousand thousands served him, and ten thousand times ten thousand stood attending him" (Daniel 7:10, NRSV).

To worship God

An angel's first and most important task is the perfect worship or the giving of love to God, who created them.

> You are the Lord, you alone; you have made heaven, the heaven of heavens, with all their host, the earth, and all that is in it, the seas and all that is in them. To all of them you give life, and the host of heaven worships you (Nehemiah 9:6, NRSV).

Psalm 148:2 says angels praise and worship God all the day long. God loves receiving love and appreciation from his creation. It should be no surprise to us that "Love himself, loves love."

To execute the program of God

Angels make up the staffing of God. God manages his universe not entrepreneurally, but corporately. He could do it all himself but created a staff to assist him. Royal guards, cherubs, seraphs, living creatures, common angels—these are all his staff members and all with a specific function. The beautiful thing about this is that they didn't have to undergo any special training; God created his angels with everything they need to do their job built in. When God says do something, everything in their being responds to his words, and they harken or respond with everything within them until they complete their task (Psalm 103:19).

To prioritize

Angels have their priorities straight—God first, everything else second. "Ascribe to the Lord, O heavenly beings, ascribe to the Lord glory and strength. Ascribe to the Lord the glory of his name; worship the Lord in holy splendor" (Palm 29:1-2).

To carry messages one-way

Angels only deliver messages one way. They deliver God's messages to us, but never our messages to God. God wants to personally hear our prayers like the tender loving Father that he is, and then he sends his angels with answers to our prayers. There are no instances in the Bible of prayer offered directly to angels. Always we pray to God and he sends his answer through his angels.

To execute judgment

The Bible says that throughout history angels have worked to carry out God's judgments, directing the destinies of nations that are displeasing to God. For example, God used angels in bringing about judgment on Sodom and Gomorrah (Genesis 18:20) and eventually on Nineveh. Furthermore, Revelation tells us that at the end of this age angels will execute judgment on those who have rejected God's love.

The writer of Hebrews speaks of angelic forces as executors of God's judgment. In 1:7 he says God "makes his angels spirits, and his ministers a flame of fire." The flaming fire suggests how awful are the judgments of God and how burning is the power of the angels who carry out God's decisions (Daniel 7:10).

Angels administer judgment in accordance with God's principles of righteousness. These mighty executors of judgment are not wimpy babies that you see in the church Christmas pageants. They are empowered by God Almighty to gather God's elect or those receiving Jesus as their Savior, and they will separate the wheat (God's children) from the tares or weeds (those destined to hell). In Matthew 13:41-42 Jesus reiterates how the angels will pull out the wicked and cast them into hell. A little later in this same chapter Jesus explains—just in case we didn't get it the first time—how angels will separate the wicked from the just and throw the wicked into hell (Matthew 13:49-50).

In addition, Revelation tells us an angel will blow the trumpet that announces impending judgment when God summons the nations to stand before him in the last great judgment. We are not called upon to obey the voice of angels. We are to heed and obey the word of God and the voice of God that calls upon us to be reconciled to him by faith in Jesus Christ. If we don't, we will have to pay the penalty of rejecting God's love—God's sacrifice through Jesus Christ, and we will have to pay the penalty for unforgiven sin. The angels will administer that penalty.

Mighty warrior angels will be involved in the judgments mentioned in the book of Revelation from chapter 4 through 19. These chapters give us a picture of the judgments to befall the earth, such as the world has never known. Angels will be involved in all of these judgments. But after these terrifying events, Christ will come with his holy angels to set up his kingdom.

To merge time into eternity

At the end of the judgments, says Billy Graham in his angel book,

> God will use angels to merge time into eternity, creating a new kind of life for every creature. Angels will also accompany Christ when he returns and will gather all things out of the new kingdom that are an offense and work iniquity, that they might be judged of sin.

Chapter Five

The Role of Angels With Mankind

The following stories address three roles angels play in relation to mankind—encouragement, protection, and carrying us to heaven. We will define and discuss these aspects later in the chapter. I believe they were given these roles because God in his mercy knew we were not able to protect ourselves from the devil on earth or on our way to heaven, so he has his wonderful and powerful angels protect us. Here are the stories.

An encouraging word (by Debra K. Matthews)

I had grown up believing that I would never amount to anything. Now at age 20 I found myself standing on an eight-foot ladder, attempting to do something I had convinced myself years before I couldn't do.

About a month before, I had been chatting with my pastor outside an old theater. It had signs on the door and in the display windows identifying it as the *Tacoma Crusade Center*, but the marquee was empty. As we talked about the history of the center, my pastor mentioned they'd never had the money to get the center's name painted on the marquee. Without thinking, I said, "I can do it."

I was shocked that I had said it. *Sure, Deb. Just like*

*that, this guy's going to up and let you paint giant letters
on his marquee. You've never even done anything that big
before. What are you thinking?*

I was committed now. Before he could say anything, I
said, "I painted the emblem on my car door," nodding my
head towards my station wagon parked at the curb beside
us. "I could paint your marquee for you."

He stepped over to look at my car door, where I had
painted a large eight-color symbol similar to the patch I
had designed for my Civil Air Patrol squadron. It had a
big eagle in flight carrying a CB radio antenna with
lightning bolts emitting from it, over a big "S" in the
background, and a scroll above and below it. The one I
had created for my squadron had said, "Pride In Our
Teamwork." But for my own personal emblem on my car I
had designed it in the shape of a shield, added a large
brown cross in the back of it all, and written, "In God We
Trust." I had painted it with a great deal of love and
pride.

My pastor looked at it for a minute, and then said,
"That's very good. How much could you do our sign for?"

"I'd do it for free," I said. "I've been wanting to do
something for you folks but didn't know if there was
anything I could do to help."

So we agreed on the job, and over the next few weeks
I painted a little each day before going to work, and
eventually got the whole thing painted with a navy blue
background and large white letters. When it was done, I
went across the street to look at the finished product, but
felt it was missing something. *It looks kind of flat*, I
thought. *Maybe I should paint a black shadow effect on
the letters.*

After drawing a picture with the shadow effect
added, I decided to do it. I painted the shadow on the first
word and then walked across the street to see how it
looked. It had made all the difference in the world. *All*

right! I went back up on the ladder and kept going. I had finished the *C-R-U-* and was carefully following the curve of the *S* when suddenly I had a scary thought. One thing about drawing as a child was that I always had to brace my arm on my desk when I drew. I couldn't work like painters and have my arm up in the air and just paint free-flow curving lines. Now, as I was painting the curve of the lower part of the *S*, I had my arm off the sign and was smoothly and exactly following the curve.

All this time while painting the letters, I had thought of it as a cut-and-dried business of filling in simple boxes and curves, not as *art or drawing.* Now, as I found the brush moving freely in this large curving line, I suddenly thought, *Maybe I* can *still draw.*

Suddenly, from below me, a voice said, "Well, I see someone is *still* an artist."

I looked down. "What?" An elderly man stood just a few feet to the left of my ladder, pulling one of those little wire carts you often see older ladies walking home with after shopping.

The man looked up at me with a smile and said, "Anyone who can draw without the paint dripping is *still* an artist." I looked up at the black line I had just painted so perfectly, and then looked down again. The man was gone! I stepped down a few rungs so I could see under the marquee, but I couldn't find him anywhere. There was no way he could have left that quickly. The businesses on both sides of the theater wouldn't be opened for hours and were locked up tight. He had simply disappeared!

I was so amazed I just stared at the big *S* in front of me. Why had he said *still* an artist, after I had just thought maybe I can *still* draw. And how could he just disappear like that? This was the third time in less than two years something unexplainable like that had hap-pened. Could it really be that the Creator of the whole earth would care enough about someone like me to send an angel to give a simple word of encouragement?

Now, years later, whenever I'm tempted to doubt that God cares about the little things in our lives, all I have to do is remember that little incident on the ladder, and I know without a shadow of a doubt, *Yes, God loves us and cares about every detail of our lives.*

The angels took my son home to heaven (by Phyllis Hotchkiss)

The evening of June 24, 1989, my 19-year-old son Brian went out with a friend. I really didn't want him to go with this person because I had a real bad feeling about him. Brian hugged and kissed me and said, "Don't worry, Mom, I will be home early." His last words before going out the door were, "I love you, Mom."

A mother never sleeps until she knows her children are home safe in bed, no matter how old they are. About midnight, I dozed off and had a dream that Brian and I were at Disney World and were on the "It's a Small World" ride, which is one of our favorites. The ride stopped and we got off, only Brian walked away from me. In my dream I saw two angels on each side of Brian, and they were taking him away from me. I had a very sick feeling.

All of a sudden like a bolt of electricity I sat straight up in bed. I looked at the clock. It was 1 a.m. Brian had not returned home. The next morning two police officers came to our door. Brian had been murdered by the friend, and robbed of his wallet for a few dollars. The friend needed money for gas for his car.

The death certificate said the time of Brian's death was 1 a.m. The time I sat straight up in bed. Did I really see angels escorting Brian to heaven? Was it a sign? I believe it was. Do I believe in angels? Most certainly. I can feel them wherever I go, and it is a very good feeling to know that someone is always there to watch over, help, and protect us.

Why didn't they protect Brian that night? What happened to Brian was an act of man not God. Angels were there to take him to heaven, where someday he will be greeting me. Although it is very difficult for any parent to have to bury a child, I found that my faith in God is what kept me going.

Angels on our side (by Kenneth Copeland)

"We see examples of what angels can do all through the Bible. When the children of Israel were fleeing from Egypt with Pharaoh's army hot on their heels, the Bible tells us that suddenly the wheels on the Egyptians' chariots just quit rolling! Who do you think was the cause of that? Angels, of course! And they haven't retired since then either. Angels are at work today just like they've always been.

"Several years ago in one of Israel's major wars, the enemy had their guns trained on Israeli compounds. Those guns were the finest military equipment money could buy. They had a range of at least 20 miles and were equipped with electronic gunsights for accuracy.

"But something very odd happened. Every time they fired those guns at the Israelis, they missed their targets, in some cases, at almost point blank range. We know there was nothing wrong with the guns because later the Israelis captured them and fired them back at the enemy with perfect success.

"What happened? Angels, that's what! In another instance, an Israeli patrol composed of just a handful of men captured 600 motorized infantrymen and all of their tanks. Why would any modern-day army surrender to such a small patrol? Because they said they heard a massive army approaching. They thought they were outnumbered! What did they actually hear? They heard angels."

As these three stories illustrate, the relationship angels have with mankind is multifaceted and complex. Let's break it down and see if we can clarify what we can expect angels to do for us.

Bring answers to our prayers

The angels' number-one relationship with mankind is to bring answers to our prayers from God, and their guardian role is a close second. But angels only deliver messages one-way. They deliver God's messages to us, but never our messages to God. God wants to personally hear our prayers like the tender loving Father that he is, and then sends his angels with answers to our prayers.

Angels attend or bring answers to our prayers, but God attends or responds personally to us when we praise and worship him.

Our prayers are heard by God, but the answer always involves the ministry of angels. This is the avenue God has chosen to work through. It's not that he couldn't answer each and every one of our prayers himself, but he has given this job to his holy angels to perform.

In the Old Testament, we see in the book of Daniel two instances where angels were sent with answers to Daniel's prayers. The first was in Daniel 10:12-14. After 21 days of prayer and fasting, a dazzling angel came to Daniel and said essentially, "We heard your prayer and tried to come with the answer the first day you prayed, but we came upon evil resistance and Michael came and helped me to get through."

Another example is in Daniel 9:20. Again Daniel had be praying and fasting for an answer from God, and Gabriel came and told him that he was going to give him the skill and understanding he needed to get his answer.

In the New Testament we see the angels attending to prayers again in Acts 12:5-10. The people were praying to God for Peter who was in jail for preaching the gospel of

Jesus Christ. Suddenly the angel came into the locked prison cell and led Peter away to freedom.

Angels are limited in power. They excel in strength (Psalm 103) but are not omnipotent. Only God is omnipotent or all-powerful. There are, however, billions of angels available to get the answers to our prayers to us. Even more important is our need to understand that angels attend to prayer and God attends to praise. While it is good to get answers to your prayers from angels, it is far better to get your answers from God through praise (Psalm 22:3).

Praise is superior to prayer, because when you praise God, you are dealing with God directly—God inhabits the praises of his people—which is far superior to getting your answer through angels. I'm not saying that we should stop praying, but we should also set aside praise time. We shouldn't just have prayer warriors. We should also have praise warriors, because praise brings the presence of God.

You will never see the Prince of Persia hold up God. Again not downplaying the importance of prayer, but God is greater than angels. Look at an example of what God does to his enemies in Psalm 68:1-2, which says, "Let God arise and let his enemies be scattered." The wicked perish at the presence of God. So if you want your prayers answered by God himself, praise him! God attends to praise personally.

Praise is understanding how much God loves you and thanking him for all the things he has done in the past and for what he will do in the future. In Acts 16:25 Paul and Silas were praying, and suddenly they switched to praising God so loudly that the other prisoners heard them. When you praise God, you don't have to worry about something holding up God. Look at what happened in verse 26. "Suddenly there was an earthquake." When God moves, things tremble. The Bible also says that the foundations were shaken, the doors opened, and the bands were loosed. When the angels rescued Peter, the doors opened, but when God came on the scene with Paul, he shook up the place.

Psalm 114:4,6-7 speaks of this same trembling earth at the presence of the Lord God of Jacob. Psalm 18:3 also tells us to call on the Lord by praise, and when we do, in verse 7 we see the same earth-and-foundation-shaking response to the presence of God. So, don't just pray. Praise the Lord!

Serve the heirs of salvation

Hebrews 1:14 comforts us when it says if you are forgiven of your sins through faith in the shed blood of Jesus on the cross, then you are an heir of salvation, saved from the penalty of sin, and you have eternal life. With this salvation comes one or more angels that are assigned to protect and direct us by God.

If you are not saved (not a Christian), the holy Scriptures give no basis for assuming that you will have any of God's angels to count on. God's angels are available to those who are saved or will be saved (remember God knows your end from the beginning). These angels are not available to the general public. Babies are generally considered to have angelic protection until they reach the age of accountability in which they are cognitively mature enough to understand the gospel, the good news that belief in Jesus brings salvation.

While doing research for this book, I read hundreds of stories describing angel sightings and encounters. Many stretch even the wildest imagination and go beyond the boundaries of what Scripture allows as being reliable. Some books promote praying directly to angels, teaching that they will respond to our prayers. But the Scripture gives no indication or instance of people even asking God to send them an angel's protection. If someone claims to have seen an angel, yet that person professes no allegiance to Jesus Christ, it's likely that the angel he saw was a fallen angel of Satan. Not every angel is from God.

Magazine articles about angels or people with stories claiming to have seen angels that have no Kingdom of God purpose are not of God. If the magazine article or the person's story—no matter how good it makes you feel—if it is not related to God accomplishing his purposes on the earth, it is not of God. God is not interested in you being "touched by an angel." He is interested in you finding the "highway to heaven."

Who are the ones destined to inherit salvation? The Bible makes it clear that this refers only to those who come to know Jesus Christ. Those are the only ones God's angels serve.

Rejoice over our salvation

Even though personal redemption is not for the angels to enjoy, they do get excited about it on our behalf. Jesus says, "There is rejoicing in the presence of the angels of God over one sinner who repents" (Luke 15:10). It sets off a heavenly party when someone responds to the call to accept Jesus as their personal Savior.

Revelation 5: 9-14 gives a fabulous picture of angelic joy over our salvation and points clearly to what may be the deepest reason for their elation. In this passage the twenty-four elders are praising Jesus, when suddenly their worship is joined by "the voice of many angels numbering thousands upon thousands, and ten thousand times ten thousand." Their praise centers on this: the entrance into God's holy heaven of those who don't deserve to be there, all through the blood of the murdered Son of God.

The angels are astonished that Jesus, God himself, would take on human flesh, and if that wasn't enough, would allow his flesh to be beaten, his back to be striped with whips, and then his body hung on a cross. I can almost hear the angels saying, "This redemption and rescue of human beings from the clutches of sin and Satan demands our eternal attention and unceasing contemplation."

Observe us

Does it seem surprising that the angels in heaven are up there watching something other than God—that they are watching us? It shouldn't, because the apostle Paul tells us in 1 Corinthians 4:9 that the apostles were on display "as a spectacle to the whole universe, to angels and to men." Paul takes this thought a step farther while instructing his assistant Timothy when he said, "In the sight of God and Christ Jesus and the elect angels" (1 Timothy 5:21).

And again Paul speaking to Timothy says that Jesus "was seen by angels" (1 Timothy 3:16). Paul had a strong sense that angels are watching everything about us now and will be watching us until the End at the time of the judgment day (Luke 12:8-9). When that day comes, what do you want the audience of angels to see and hear about you?

"That angels are watching over us, should encourage and strengthen us," Billy Graham believes. According to Graham, angels are watching us, marking our paths, superintending the events of our lives, and protecting the interests of God. They are always working to promote the Lord's plans and to bring about his highest will for us. Angels are interested spectators and mark all we do. God assigns angelic powers to watch over us as they did over Hagar, Sarah's maid in Genesis 16:7. We see their protective role in Psalm 34:7, "The angel of the Lord encamps around those who fear God and delivers them."

Show us how to worship God

In his book *Somewhere Angels*, Larry Libby tells children and their parents about some of the things we can learn from angels. One of them is, "We can learn how to worship the Lord with all our hearts." Angels worship not only wholeheartedly, but also all the time, Libby says. He suggests, "I think angels have been worshiping from the time they first opened their eyes and saw God's smile."

There are even special angels around God's throne who never, ever stop praising his name. They don't have rest time or recess. They don't go home at night, because there is no night—and they wouldn't want to leave God's side even if there was. Shouting and singing praise to the Lord is all they do—and all they want to do—forever and ever.

Jesus spoke of angels who "always see the face of my Father in heaven" (Matthew 18:10). The angels' unbroken gaze upon the face of God stimulates lots of rich, genuine worship. We could learn this very fact from them—to keep our gaze upon the face of God who is in our heart and to have a lifestyle of continuous praise and worship. Just as the apostle Paul told us to pray without ceasing, I feel we are to do the same and worship God without ceasing also. Like the angels we should also live in the presence of God and stay focused on God through praise and worship.

Carry the saints to heaven

Angels are present when God's children die. People do die, but not all go to heaven. I have been a registered nurse for over twenty years, and for thirteen of those years I worked as a cancer nurse. I've ministered to those who were dying. I've been with them in the process, and I've been in the room after the death has occurred. I've watched their loved ones mourn over their loss, trying to hold on to a body where there was no longer any life.

There is something that happens in the process between seeing people hold on to life one minute and seeing them with no life the next. I believe, based on the Scriptures, that angels take believers home to heaven when we die. This fact is a comfort to many in that they can be assured that their loved one did not cross that great divide alone but was escorted into the presence of the Most High God by one of the angels. Remember Andrew, the angel of death on the popular television show *Touched by an Angel*? This was his job, and we saw him guide the children of God into heaven, smiling and laughing along the way—sorry to leave, but happy to be going to heaven.

I believe this is true. I've seen unbelievers die, and it is not a pretty sight. They gasp for every breath, a strained, open-mouth expression, a furrowed brow, a tear rolling down their cheek for all the sins they knew they committed but were not forgiven for, or perhaps they are seeing the place reserved for evil angels and unbelievers—hell. Some unbelievers even cry out at the time of death—No, no, no. Only God knows what they are seeing.

On the other hand, when a believer—one who knows their sins are forgiven and that they have eternal life—is dying, there is no stress, their face is relaxed, a slight smile, a prayer or song on their lips, a prayer for a loved one to be strong, a word of encouragement that they will see them again in heaven, praise and worship music in the background. Some have even said, "I'm coming, Jesus." Many children when they are about to die see the angels that are to escort them and may even talk to them. Believers are happy and relaxed because they know that this isn't the end for them. It's the beginning of their eternity with God. So, when they die, there is a holy rejoicing in the room. The unbelieving nurses are amazed at what they see and hear—not tears and grief, but smiles and the praising of God.

My observations as a cancer nurse agree with Billy Graham's theory on what happens to the saints when they die. In his book on angels, Graham says death is not natural for man. Man was created to live forever and not to die. Death is the result of God's judgment because of man's sin and rebellion in the Garden of Eden.

Graham believes that at the moment of death the spirit departs from the body and moves through the atmosphere. The Scripture also tells us that the devil lurks there, because he is the "prince of the power of the air" (Ephesians 2:2). If our spiritual eyes could be open, we would probably see the air filled with evil angels, the enemies of Christ. If Satan could hinder the angel of Daniel 10 for three weeks on his mission to earth, imagine the opposition a Christian would encounter at death.

The moment of death is Satan's final opportunity to attack the true believer, but God sends his angels to guard us and escort us during our travel through the air to heaven. The Scripture says there is a time to be born and a time to die. When the believer's time to die comes, an angel will be there to protect and comfort them.

Another argument for the belief that the saints are escorted into heaven by angels comes from the mouth of Jesus. Jesus related in Luke 16:19 the story of two men, one a beggar and one a rich man. The beggar, covered with sores and dying, begged for food at the gate of the rich man's home everyday. Finally he died and the Scripture tells us he was carried to Abraham's side (this Jewish mindset denotes a place of feasting and joy we'll know in eternity or heaven). The rich man also died and went to hell and was in torment.

The Scriptures also hint that Jesus may have been carried by angels on the day of his ascension. Mark 16:19 reads that "he was taken up into heaven." Luke writes that while Jesus was blessing his disciples, he was taken up into heaven (24:51). The King James Version reads this way: "While he blessed them, he was parted from them and was carried up into heaven." Acts 1:9 says that "after he said this, he was taken up before their very eyes." What a privilege for the angels to take up their own Creator to heaven.

In summary, we need God's angels to guide us from our temporary home here on earth to our permanent home in heaven. I agree with Larry Libby when he says, "God wants you home so much he'll send his own angel to meet you. And don't be surprised if the angel is wearing a big smile."

Protect us

Again, according to the Bible, the only people who have guardian angels are people who have accepted Jesus' redemptive work on the cross, which includes forgiveness of sins, healing of our bodies, peace of mind, and everlasting life. All these things come under the heading of salvation. But salvation is even more than this.

We must understand that the word *salvation* in Scripture does not refer simply to the eternal, go-to-heaven-when-you-die, or the new-birth kind of salvation. The Greek word translated salvation is *soteria*. If we look up the word *soteria*, we will find that it "denotes deliverance, preservation of material, and temporal deliverance." Real biblical salvation not only includes eternal protection, but also it includes protection from all the material dangers of life in the here and now.

Now, with that in mind, read Hebrews 1:14 again. "Are they [angels] not all ministering spirits, sent forth to minister for them who shall be heirs of salvation?"

Just think about that. God has created vast numbers of gloriously powerful spiritual beings for the express purpose of protecting us

> and delivering us from the evils of this world—
> from everything from hurricanes to plane
> crashes, and from gang violence to AIDS
> (Kenneth Copeland, *Angels on Your Side*)

It is comforting to know that the Lord has given his angels charge over us, and they will keep us in all our ways (Psalm 91:11).

Angels often protect or rescue us by leading us out of harm's way. Angels may see the big picture, but they never overlook the smallest details. "The angel tapped Peter on the side and woke him, saying, 'Get up quickly.' And the chains fell off of his wrists. The angel said to him, 'Wrap your cloak around you and follow me'" (Acts 12:7-8, NRSV). The angel certainly was concerned about getting him out of jail, but he also wanted him to be warm along the way.

We have many Bible examples of how the Lord rescues his saints from potential harm. In 2 Kings 6:14-17, the king of Syria had sent out his army to Dothan after learning that Elisha the prophet was there. Upon dressing one morning, Elisha's helper exclaimed to Elisha that there was a vast army on the surrounding country-side with implements of war. Elisha told his servant not to be afraid, because an army bigger than this one was here to protect them. Elisha prayed to the Lord to open his servant's eyes so that he could see this also. The Lord opened his eyes and he could see a host of protective angels with horses and chariots of fire on the hills surrounding the city.

This passage has been a great comfort to me in times of trouble. It even prompted me to start my innumerable angel figurine collection so that I could have a continuous visual reminder that the angels of the Lord are all around me protecting me. They're the same mighty angels that protected Elisha and his servant.

Act as a matchmaker

If you are single, one of the jobs of an angel is to find you a mate. In Genesis 24:7 Abraham wants a bride for his son Isaac and sends his servant to find one. But before his servant leaves, Abraham tells him that God will send an angel before him to find a wife for his son. The angel leads Abraham's servant to Rebekah. Rebekah meets the qualifications, comes back, and marries Isaac on the spot.

Bring us messages from God

If an angel gives you a message, act on it at once. "When Joseph awoke from sleep, he did as the angel of the Lord commanded him" (Matthew 1:24).

Teach us

Our angels are patient tutors appointed by a loving, caring Parent to teach us and guide us along the paths of wisdom.

> When I, Daniel, had seen the vision, I tried to understand it. Then someone appeared standing before me, having the appearance of a man, and I heard a man's voice between the banks of Ulai, which called, and said, Gabriel, help this man understand the vision (Daniel 8:15-16, NRSV with KJV).

Remember those superior angelic communication skills we talked about earlier? They really come in handy when they are trying to teach us something.

Strengthen us

An angel's function is not to do our work for us, but to help us to do it ourselves, by God's grace. Jesus prayed, "Father if you are willing, remove this cup from me; yet not my will but yours be done. Then an angel from heaven appeared to him and gave him strength"

(Luke 22:42-43). In the Old Testament, Daniel grew weak and faint when he was in the presence of archangel Gabriel.

> Again one in human form touched me and strengthened me. He said, "Do not fear, greatly beloved, you are safe. Be strong and courageous!" When he spoke to me, I was strengthened and said, "Let my Lord speak, for you have strengthened me" (Daniel 10:18-19, NRSV).

As Daniel surely knew, Gabriel means "Strong One of God," and we are all Gabriels when we lean on the Lord for strength.

Many times in the Old and New Testaments people cried out to God and received their deliverance either by God helping them directly or through angels acting on their behalf. God's ministering angels are the calm assurance that we can have while facing the cataclysms of life. While we do not place our faith directly in angels, we should place it in the God who rules the angels; then we can have peace and strength.

Won't accept some things from us

Biblical angels will not accept anything from us beyond simple regard and gratitude. Everything else they lay before God. "The angel of the Lord said to Manoah, 'If you detain me, I will not eat your food, but if you want to prepare a burnt offering, then offer it to the Lord'" (Judges 13:16). God's angels always point men back to God.

1. Disobedience

When Elizabeth's husband did not believe the angel, he was struck dumb until John the Baptist was born and named according to the angel's instructions (Luke 1:20). Lot's wife turned to a pillar of salt when she disobeyed and looked back at Sodom and Gomorrah (Genesis 19:26).

2. Worship

Satan is a constant reminder of what happens to angels when they accept the praises of human beings. When the apostle John wanted to worship an angel in Revelation 19:10 and 22:9, the angel essentially said, "No, don't do that," and proceeded to tell him that he was "a fellow servant with the brothers who hold to the testimony of Jesus." Even though God's angels are powerful and wonderful beings, we should not get too excited about them. Colossians 2:1 cautions, "Let no man beguile you of your reward in a voluntary humility and worshiping of angels."

Are persistent until we do the will of God

Elijah "lay down under the broom tree and fell asleep. Suddenly an angel touched him and said, 'Get up and eat' . . . He ate and drank and lay down again. The angel of the Lord came again and said, 'Get up and eat, otherwise the journey will be too much for you.' He got up and ate and drank; then he went in the strength of that food forty days and forty nights" (1 Kings 19:4-7, NRSV).

Can't be fooled

The [angel of the] Lord said to Abraham,
> Why did Sarah laugh and say, "Shall I indeed bear a child now that I am old?" Is anything too wonderful for the Lord? . . ." But Sarah denied, saying, "I did not laugh"; for she was afraid. He said, "Oh yes, you did laugh" (Genesis 18:13-15, NRSV).

As we already know, angels are very wise and have God-given supernatural abilities beyond what we can comprehend.

Help us to succeed

Whenever you have an important meeting, always

pray to God that the other person's angel keeps the lines of communication open. "The Lord, before whom I walk, will send his angel with you and make your way successful" (Genesis 24:40, NRSV).

Clarify things

Again, God's angels are perfect communicators. They always make certain we understand their messages. "[Gabriel] said to me, Daniel, greatly beloved, pay attention to the word that I am going to speak to you. Stand to your feet, for I have now been sent to you" (Daniel 10:11, NRSV).

Don't like it when we do wrong

Our angels always love us, but when we do hurtful things, they probably don't like us very much. "The angel of the Lord said to [Balaam], 'Why have you struck your donkey these three times. I have come out as an adversary, because your way is perverse before me'" (Numbers 22:32, NRSV).

Activating angelic help

In order to receive help from God's angels, we have to get ourselves in the right position for his angels to come and help us. First we must be children of God who have accepted Jesus as our Lord and the salvation and eternal life that comes with it.

Next, we must exercise our faith and get our words and actions in line with God's word by daily Bible reading. Why? Because, according to Psalm 103:20, God's word is what sets the angels in motion: "Bless the Lord, ye his angels, that excel in strength, that do his commandments, hearkening unto the voice of his word."

When we're in trouble, we should speak God's word, and not talk about how awful things are. Speak the word of God. Give your angel something to respond to! Say,

I am an heir of salvation. I am an heir of
preservation and deliverance. The angels are
ministering spirits sent forth to minister that
deliverance for me. And, Father God, in the
Name of Jesus, I'm asking you to be true to
your words in the Bible and send your angels
to help me.

Once you've spoken that word of faith, stand fast.
Don't waiver. Give the angels time to work! They're real
beings, and you've given them a real job to do.

When we've done these things, we must not fear but
believe that greater is God who is in us than the devil
who is in the world. We should continue to stand in faith,
knowing that God can deliver us out of any situation and
that nothing is impossible for God. Our faith will get
stronger and stronger as we abide or live on a day-to-day
basis in the presence of the Most High God through
prayer and meditation on the holy Scriptures. Now that
we're in the right position to receive godly angelic help in
our lives, let's look at how we can jumpstart them into
action.

That there is a specific way to activate God's angels
to work in our behalf should not be that hard to believe.
An analogy of this is the specific way we must activate a
credit card. The credit card company tells us exactly how
to activate it, because we can't activate the card without
following their exact directions. And if we don't activate
the card, we can't use it because we can't draw out money
against it for goods and services.

And once it's activated, we have to use it the right
way. For example, when we're at a gas station trying to
get gas, if we don't put the card in the right way, it won't
activate. So it is with the activation of angels; we have to
activate them the right way. Otherwise they will not
work in our behalf.

In our discussion on positioning ourselves so that

God can allow his angels to work on our behalf, we were not talking about asking angels directly to help us, but through prayer to God. Jesus is the holy angels' boss, and Satan is the evil angels' boss. We are not the employer of any of them. So we don't have any authority to ask them for anything on our own. The authority comes because as believers, we are in a right relationship with God. Therefore he is predisposed to designate angelic activity on our behalf.

So activation is just following the correct chain of command. In a business, if we have a problem, we go to our direct supervisor about it first. God is our direct and only supervisor, and we should go to him first with all our problems. As with our supervisors at work, he will delegate the task of taking care of our problems to the angels. It's as simple as that.

CHAPTER SIX

Demonology

We have included this chapter on demons, because even though demons are not angels, they are directly controlled by Satan, who is an evil angel. They are the workhorses of the dark world. The evil angels work behind the scenes and let the demons do their dirty work on the earth.

In this chapter we will look more closely at where they come from, their personhood, their doctrines, and how we can protect ourselves from demonic activity in our lives. But, before we get started, let's look at a true story about the activity of a demon in the lives of a group of teenagers. Entitled "The Demon of Wilderness Creek," this story is by an unknown author, but it appeared on web site Paranormalphenomenon.com. The story presents the reality of demons and affirms the only cure for demonic possession and oppression, Jesus Christ. In this true story, five Oklahoma teenagers' attendance to a Southern Baptist youth camp began a terrifying conflict with a demon named Eza.

The Demon of Wilderness Creek
Nestled deep in the Arbucle Mountains of Oklahoma is the isolated retreat of Wilderness Creek. Known for its

beautiful, lush scenery, Wilderness Creek is a densely wooded area veined by an inviting boulder-strewn creek that provides the perfect setting for a youth camp. Every summer kids from several congregations gather at the campgrounds for fun, exercise, fellowship, and Bible instruction. For Ami and a few friends, however, the summer of 1995 marked the beginning of a terrifying episode in their lives.

This was Ami's first summer at Wilderness Creek. She was there with several friends, all of them about 14 years old, including Sherry, Anne, and Mandy.

Everything was great for the first few days, says Ami, until it came time for the Wednesday night tabernacle. It was a warm June evening when the kids gathered for their usual evening's hour of ministry and prayer. But there was one uninvited guest at the meeting.

Standing about 35 feet from the tabernacle was a boy no one had ever seen at the camp before. Byron was the first to notice him. The strange boy seemed to be about 17 or 18 years old and was dressed in all black. Byron pointed fearfully at him. He was then seen by Ami, Anne, Mandy, and Sherry. He had black hair, was wearing black pants and a black sweater, which I thought odd for a warm summer night.

Upon seeing him, the youths immediately fell ill. Ami, Mandy, and Byron had trouble breathing. Sherry doubled over with stomach pain. Anne's pains could have been a sign of something far worse. All the youth leaders saw that something was seriously wrong with these kids and rushed the five to the camp's infirmary. Even though he was at the point of coughing up blood, Byron was told he had asthmatic bronchitis. Bronchitis was also blamed for Ami and Mandy's breathing problems. Sherry told the staff she was experiencing the worse stomach pain of her life. Anne had worse problems, because she feared she was pregnant and that her pains meant she was having a miscarriage. While the other kids were treated at the infirmary, Anne was rushed out of Wilderness Creek to a nearby hospital.

The five kids made no mention of the strange boy in black that they had seen near the tabernacle, and no one else—neither the other campers nor the adult leaders—seemed to have noticed him.

Byron was especially troubled by these strange events, as if he knew more than he was letting on. As soon as he was released from the infirmary he ran off into the dark. When given the okay to leave the infirmary, Ami, Mandy, and Sherry headed for their bunkhouse.

By the time the girls got back to their bunks, Anne had already returned from the hospital but was kept in a separate room. Byron was there looking pale and ill-at-ease. Sherry left the bunkhouse to go speak to one of the youth leaders and Ami sat beside Byron on the bunk and asked him why he looked like he'd seen a ghost.

At first it was difficult for Byron to speak. The words seemed to catch in his throat. Slowly he told her about the boy in black.

The boy in black was not a boy at all, but a demon named Eza, Byron told her. Byron confided that he had been possessed by Eza at various times in the last few years. Eza would demand that Byron do certain things for him and, if he refused, the demon simply took control of Byron's body.

Ami sat in silent disbelief. Byron was probably still suffering from the effects of the illness he had, she thought. Either that or he's just plain nuts. Being raised in a fundamentalist faith, Ami was taught that demons were real spiritual entities who could manifest themselves and take control of a human being, but to do it to one of her friends was inconceivable. Byron then asked Ami not to reveal his secret to anyone else, and she agreed.

The remaining days at the camp seemed normal. Ami rationalized that the episode was probably a result of heat and exhaustion. The alternative was just too unreal. As the normality of the following days filled the kids' lives, the incident was almost forgotten.

A few months later when Ami was home, the summer season was winding down and she was spending time with her cousin before school started again. While idly enjoying each other's company in Ami's bedroom, her cousin looked out the window and she saw someone in her backyard. Ami immediately thought of Byron. She hadn't seen him since camp, but he had phoned her recently and said he would be coming over. That's probably him in the backyard fooling around. Playfully, Ami pretended not to hear. But before the game could continue, she heard a voice.

It spoke to her as if it were standing right next to her. Ami was so shocked and frightened by this disembodied voice that she was thrown into a kind of delirium. In that wild moment of unreality, Ami believed that she was pregnant and that this voice was going to kill her baby. Then almost as quickly as it struck, the dread feeling faded, Ami awoke to the reality that this threat was an impossibility. She was after all, still a virgin.

Ami explained to her cousin what had just happened. The girls like many young teens, were fascinated by witchcraft and the idea that a kind of magic or control over one's surroundings and circumstances was a real possibility. Together they decided to perform a "seeing ritual" to see if they could discover the root cause of the bizarre thing that had just happened. A seeing ritual, Ami had read, was a ritual that reveals truth to the mind of the caster. Whatever is hidden, whether a lie or someone in the shadows, the truth will be shone.

The ritual had effects far more intense than either girl expected, however. The two girls fell into a state of unconsciousness or super-consciousness, and shared a vision. "We saw Eza, dressed the same as he was at Wilderness Creek, standing in the middle of a fork in the road," Ami recalls. "On one side the path looked rather inviting. It was lit and looked like a spring day, but on the other side, the trees were twisted and it was night. You could hear the noises on the dark side, but on the light side it was eerily quiet. Without opening his mouth, Eza told us we could choose either path, and he would let us walk without coming near us.

"Neither of us knew what to do, and then it changed. We were no longer together. In my vision, since I can't remember hers, I was walking down the hall in my home and then into my room." Standing in the doorway of her room, in the vision, Ami saw her cousin and herself sitting together on her bed, as they likely were in reality. They both looked at the Ami standing in the doorway. Suddenly, her cousin sitting on the bed grabbed Ami by the neck and broke it, smiling gleefully.

At that instant, both girls awoke from their trances, feeling frightened and confused. They compared the experiences of their visions, and it was then that her cousin knew, without being told, what had happened at Wilderness Creek. Overwhelmed with the intensity of the moment, the cousins were nearly startled out of their wits when the doorbell ran. It was Byron.

Byron was with his friend, Brandy, and Ami invited them in. She told him that of the experience they'd had with Eza. "I know," Byron said. Eza had been tormenting him, Byron told them, urging Byron to sexually attack the girls because he wanted the purity of virgins. Byron said he resisted Eza and refused to do his bidding. Brandy then mentioned that she had heard that some demons could in fact rape a person without the aid of a human body. Ami had never heard of this and didn't believe Brandy's incredible claim.

At that point, Byron lay on the floor and called Eza into him. But Ami was getting fed up with all this bizarre nonsense, suspecting that Byron was just playing with their minds. As Byron approached Ami, she handed him a Bible. Byron screamed and dropped the book on the floor, crying that it had burned his hands. Ami was now becoming irritated by Byron's act . . . until she looked at her Bible, which bore the marks of Byron's handprint. They remained on the cover, Ami said, for several days and then disappeared.

Over the next week, Ami continued to experience some strange phenomenon while playing with a Ouija board. All it would do is spell out *Eza*. And when asked what it wanted, the pointer would move clearly toward Ami. She also saw some hallucinations while falling asleep and had some wicked dreams, but they all soon passed.

Ami has not seen Byron since that last meeting at her house. "The last I heard, about two days before all of it stopped for me, was that he was going to go to some kind of white magic ritual and have the demons cast out," she said.

As for Ami, she has turned her back on all aspects of the occult. "I don't believe in witchcraft anymore," she said. "I'm a Christian now. I believe that my turn to God at that time saved me. I am guessing that unless Byron has gotten saved in the last four and one half years, Eza is still with him."

Now that we know that demons are real and can enter into our lives unexpectedly—even at a Christian youth camp, let's look a little closer at the subject of demons.

Demons: The race on the earth before Adam

To know where any class of spiritual being comes

from, we have to go back to the beginning, to God.

Genesis 1:1 tells us, "In the beginning God created the heavens and the earth." God is the beginning and is before all things. While we are discussing this, keep in mind that the Bible speaks of three heavens: Genesis 1:8 speaks of the atmosphere, the second heaven is mentioned in Ephesians 6 where principalities and powers are, and the third heaven where Paul saw God is in 2 Corinthians 12:2.

That God created the heavens, which includes the angels which inhabit them, is validated in Job 38:4 and Psalm 104:4. These two Scriptures relay the thought that the angels were already on the scene when God created the earth. All the angels in God's heaven are good angels. So where did bad angels and demons come from?

I agree with Pastor and Evangelist Benny Hinn's theory discussed in his tape series, "War in the Heavenlies." Hinn asserts that demons are not the same as evil angels, but that they are two entirely different beings. He feels that demons were the pre-Adamic race, or the race on the earth before Adam's or mankind's creation and at the time of Lucifer's rebellion and fall from heaven. The following discussion is based on his theory.

Genesis 1:1 tells us, "In the beginning God created the heavens and the earth." Genesis 1:2 says, "And the earth was without form, and void." Something took place between verses 1 and 2. The earth became void. Why? What happened?

I agree with Hinn who says,. "Billions of years exist between Genesis 1:1 and 1:2," and this is where the fall of Lucifer (a.k.a. Satan or the devil) occurred. Also, during that period was the destruction of the earth and its inhabitants that we know today as demons. In addition, when Lucifer fell, so did the one third of heavens angels who followed him, and they are now bound with chains in the underworld. There were disasters going on that we can't even imagine. The earth God created in perfection was destroyed because of the rebellion.

The following material presents proofs of the existence of a pre-Adamic race and the high probability that it was a race of demons. I would say, however, that the demons then are not the demons today. They were, as all God's creatures, created as a thing of beauty that was later defiled when they turned their allegiance from God to Satan (see the description of demons in Revelation 9:1). They went from being beautiful creatures created by God to ones of ugliness and evil after they bowed to Satan.

Proof 1: There was destruction on the earth before mankind

Job 9:5 tells us that there was a time in earth's history that God was so angry he removed the mountains and shook the earth out of the pillar of its space, commanded the sun not to shine, and sealed the stars. When did all this happen? Not in this millennium, not since Adam, and not when Jesus comes back. This is not talking about Noah's flood. It's talking about another destructive event on the earth.

Then in Job 9:8 there is the restoration verse, "Which alone spreadeth out the heavens, and treadeth upon the waves of the sea." This is almost equivalent to the one taking place in Genesis 1:2-4, "And the Spirit of God moved upon the face of the waters. And God said, Let there be light: and there was light. And God saw the light, that it was good: and God divided the light from the darkness."

Proof 2: Second reference to destruction on the earth before mankind

In Jeremiah 4:23-26, the prophet had a vision that

sounds familiar:

> I beheld the earth, and, lo, it was without
> form, and void; and the heavens, and they
> had no light. I beheld the mountains, and, lo,
> they trembled, and all the hills moved lightly.
> I beheld, and, lo, there was no man, and all
> the birds of the heavens were fled. I beheld,
> and, lo, the fruitful place was a wilderness,
> and all the cities thereof were broken down.

We know this text is addressing the condition of
Israel at that time, but it also seems to be pointing to
some other historical event. Most theological scholars
will agree the Bible often speaks on one physical situation or event while pointing to another. The most famous
of these is the Jewish celebration of Passover—when they
left slavery in the land of Egypt and passed over into
their God-promised land (see the book of Exodus). But,
before they left, the Pharaoh or king of Egypt changed his
mind about letting them go.

God told the Israelites he was going to send a de-
stroyer, who is most likely an angel, to kill the firstborn
son in every family in Egypt so that Pharaoh would let
the Jews go to their promised land. The Jews were in-
structed that if they killed a lamb and applied its blood to
the doorposts of their homes, the death angel would pass
over their house and their sons would be spared. This
was also a foreshadowing of Jesus Christ, as the Bible
calls him God's "Passover lamb" (1 Corinthians 5:7).

The Bible says that faith in his shed blood provides
forgiveness of sin and eternal life. The literal "Passover"
of the Jews as they prepared to leave Egypt we later find
was a type—a foreshadowing of a thing to come—of the
true "Passover lamb," Jesus the Christ, who gives us not
just temporary but eternal life.

Going back to Jeremiah 4:23-26, we see the same
scene found in Genesis 1:2 which says that the "earth

was without form and void." Remember how Genesis 1:1 seems to go from the positive verse 1, "God created heaven and earth," to the negative in verse 2, "The earth was without form and void." What happened?

Jeremiah 4:26 brings up even more questions, "I beheld, and, lo, the fruitful place *was* a wilderness, and all the cities thereof were broken down." All cities broken down? What cities were here before Adam? Why was God so angry? With whom was he angry? He couldn't be angry with creation. I propose God was angry with Satan, his evil angels, and the pre-Adamic race of beings on the earth at that time.

Proof 3: The pre-Adamic race was sent to the "Pit" with Lucifer

Isaiah 24:1 talks about God's wrath on the inhabitants of the earth before Adam: "Behold, the LORD maketh the earth empty, and maketh it waste, and turneth it upside down, and scattereth abroad the inhabitants thereof." We see the same emptiness of the earth in Genesis 1:2 and Jeremiah 4:23-26.

It's as if God took a full table, lifted it up and turned it upside down, scattering everything on the ground. But, when did he turn it upside down? There has not been a day since Adam that the earth was upside down. It's not going to be during the Lord's reign on earth or even after that. And, what about "scattering the inhabitants"? What inhabitants? They aren't human beings. Mankind couldn't live on an upside down world like the one described in Job, Jeremiah, or Isaiah. We would all be dead. Instead the inhabitants are still alive and running. Who is this that is upside down and scattered but still alive? Demons. They are frightened and running.

What happened that made the Lord so angry that he would turn the earth upside down? The only thing the Bible shows to really make God that mad is when someone steals his glory or in other words takes the credit and the praise for what God alone has done. This would be in line with what the Bible says Satan tried to do. He readily accepted the praise that belonged to God. In Isaiah 14:4-18 Satan presents his true intent to take over heaven as he had done with the inhabitants on the earth.

Isaiah 14:16 relates how the inhabitants of the earth at that time, who were also cast into the pit or hell with Satan looked hard at him and said, "Is this the one who fooled the nations?"

No, the Bible doesn't come out point blank and say the pre-Adamic race were demons, but by doing some scientific induction one can figure it out. Scientific induction would say, first, that the Bible only mentions four classes of spiritual beings: God, angels, demons, and man. Secondly, there was a pre-Adamic race that was fooled into committing treason against God and following Satan. Thirdly, this pre-Adamic race was sent with Satan to the pit. Lastly, the only Bible mention of creatures being in or sent to the pit are demons and Satan. There are some other evil angels in hell, but the Bible never refers to the place as the pit (Luke 8:31).

Proof 4: "Replenish the earth." The pre-Adamic race was not made in the image of God.

That mankind couldn't live in the upside down world described in Isaiah 24 is another proof of a pre-Adamic race. As a registered nurse, I know all too well that for mankind to exist, everything in the environment of the earth has to be in balance and functioning perfectly. If one thing goes out of balance, man's existence is threatened. For example, if a person's potassium level is too low, their heart won't beat right, or if the person is not able to take in enough oxygen, for whatever reason, he will die. So if the earth was upside down and ecologically unbalanced through fires, floods, and no sun, we would die and die fast. I believe that the demons survived because they were made in another image that allowed them to continue to exist in such a chaotic environment.

When God decided to create the second inhabitants of the earth, he made the creature in a better image—his image, as is written in Genesis 1:26-28,

> And God said, Let us make man in our image, after our likeness [or kind] and let them have dominion . . . So God created man in his own image, in the image of God created he him; male and female created he them. And God blessed them and said . . . be fruitful, and multiply, and replenish the earth, and subdue it.

If God made it a point to say in the Bible that he created mankind in his image, then we must conclude that the first inhabitants of the earth were of another image or species. In addition, we need to point out that God said "replenish" the earth, indicating that the earth that had once been filled was now empty, and God wanted his man to replenish it.

God wanted to replenish the earth with a different race—this time one made in his likeness or kind. I don't think it was an accident that God said that. Again, I believe he was emphasizing the fact that the first species to inhabit the earth was not of his image, but this man is. If the other species—demons—were also made in God's image, there would be no need to differentiate man.

It was important to God to make mankind like himself. I believe this was necessary for us to be able to receive fully the nature, love, and fellowship of God. As we all know, normal people can't have perfect fellowship, for example, with a dog or cat. Perfect fellowship and intimacy only come with having relationships with other people. That may have been why the other inhabitants turned away from God to Satan. Maybe they didn't have the capacity to understand the heart of God. But man would be able to know him.

So when God—Jesus—wrapped himself in the clothes of mankind, he knew once again the joy of being with his man—male and female man. To touch them, to hug them, to talk to them face to face. To look into their eyes and have them look back into his—the love of two persons face to face, hand to hand. Jesus, God, knew now that he could never stand being separated from his people again.

This is why the Garden of Gethsemane was so hard for Jesus (Matthew 26:36). This is why he prayed to God the Father about his upcoming crucifixion. To go or not to go to the cross was the question. Jesus asked himself, "Shall I go back to my Father in glorious heaven, or shall I die on the cross so that mankind can come back with me to my Father in heaven?"

As the old song goes, "Did you ever have to make up your mind? Choose one and leave the other behind." Jesus did, and he chose to provide the way for us to come back to God the Father through his death on the cross by which he paid for every past, present, and future sin we would commit. He did this because we all have sinned and fallen short of God's holy standard for entry to heaven. All we have to do is choose Jesus, who the Bible says is the way back to right standing with God.

God, who knows the end from the beginning, knew that even Adam would be fooled by Satan in the Garden of Eden and would sin by obeying Satan and not God's command. Before Adam's creation, God set in motion his plan (Revelation 13:8) to send his Son to become a man, live a sinless life, and then die on the cross for all of mankind's sins. If we turn to the Son, Jesus, we can have our sins forgiven, eternal life, and victory over every attack of the enemy, Satan.

Perhaps that is why God made man in his image,

because he knew his Son would have to come to earth and live in that image. For the Son, Jesus to fit inside a human spirit, soul, and body, there had to be a perfect match, yet still he had to be fully a man—a man able to sin and resist it in order to be a perfect sacrifice for our sins.

The Son was literally the second Adam. The second one to be created that was pure and without sin. He was tempted, except this time the Son, Jesus, did not fail. And because he was capable of sinning but did not sin, he became the perfect sacrifice for our sins. Jesus stood in our place and accepted the just consequences of all mankind's sin; past, present, and future.

What's all this about sacrificing, and why is it important? The Bible says without the shedding of blood there is no forgiveness of sin (Hebrews 9:22). And some even say, "Well, Jesus was God. That's how he resisted sin." To think like this would be like saying that God is a liar, because he said that Jesus resisted the heavy pressure of sin to the point that his sweat was like great drops of blood (Luke 22:44). As a nurse I have seen patients exude from their skin a pinkish fluid during times of great psychological or physical stressors.

But God in his mercy knew that even though we were made in his image, we would not be able to resist sin to this point, so he provided us with another way. In the Old Testament there was the sacrificing of animals for sin. This had to be done year after year to remain acceptable in God's eyes. In the New Testament we are cleansed of sin once and for all by faith in what the shed blood of Jesus accomplished on the cross.

Through faith in Jesus' blood every human being made in the image of God has their sins forgiven, victory over the devil in this life, and everlasting life in heaven with God himself. We are his children. God delights in his children being like himself. God will never again allow his enemy (not his equal) to fool his children and take them away. So after Jesus' death on the cross and his ascension to heaven, God sent his own Holy Spirit to live in the hearts of his children.

God knew that the only way his children could resist the devil was to have his Holy Spirit living in their hearts, guiding them and shedding light on the truths of God day by day. And, because we are made in God's image, the Holy Spirit fits perfectly inside us to guide, counsel, comfort, and protect us.

Proof 5: There was a devastating flood on the earth before Noah's flood

Psalm 104:1-7 verifies that the angels were created before Adam or mankind, but, it also provides biblical proof of the earth being inhabited by a pre-Adamic race because of its discussion of a flood that occurred prior to Noah's flood

> Bless the LORD, O my soul. O LORD my God, thou art very great; thou art clothed with honor and majesty. Who covereth thyself with light as with a garment: who stretchest out the heavens like a curtain. Who layeth the beams of his chambers in the waters: who maketh the clouds his chariot: who walketh upon the wings of the wind. Who maketh his angels spirits; his ministers a flaming fire. Who laid the foundations of the earth, that it should not be removed for ever. Thou covered it with the deep as with a garment: the waters stood above the mountains. At thy rebuke they fled; at the voice of thy thunder they hasted away.

What's all this talk about angels, spirits, flames, and waters? Here the Bible is talking about a pre-Adamic flood, not Noah's. It was a time when something happened on the earth that was so upsetting to God that he literally shook things up on the earth.

In the floods of Psalm 104, Job 9, and Genesis 1:2,7 the destruction and flooding is sudden by one word of rebuke by God. This couldn't have been Noah's flood, because it started and stopped gradually. First it rained for 40 days and forty nights and then stayed on the earth for 150 days and then was gradually removed.

In the pre-Adamic flood, God flooded the earth instantly, and the sun stopped and the earth became like a frozen ball of ice. Its destruction was sudden, which is in line with what science found with dinosaurs and other beast and plant life frozen suddenly. I believe that this sudden destruction and flooding came upon the earth because of Lucifer's rebellion, which involved demons, the inhabitants of the earth at that time.

Concluding thoughts

After a review of all the evidences we must conclude that there was a race of beings on the earth before mankind that committed treason against God and chose to follow Satan. After the treason, they were sent to the pit with Satan. This race of beings were demons.

Now that we understand the biblical basis for asserting that there was a pre-Adamic race of demons on the earth, we present later on in this chapter the specific differences between evil angels and demons, and show without a shadow of a doubt that bad angels and demons are not the same.

What is a demon?

As previously mentioned, I believe demons were the inhabitants of the earth in the period of Satan's rebellion. Lucifer led these inhabitants to worship him rather than leading them to God. Because of Satan's mutiny, a war ensued which resulted in the destruction of the earth and

Satan, and the demons were thrown into the pit or hell.

But I believe that demons were created beautiful like all of God's good creation, but when they chose to turn their backs on God to follow Satan, they lost their beauty and became the hideous creatures described in Revelation 9:7. In addition, the Bible does not say whether the pre-Adamic inhabitants were always called demons or whether their name was changed to demons after their act of treason, as Lucifer's was changed to Satan.

After the fall of Satan, the demons were confined to the pit or hell. Isaiah the prophet vividly describes in 14:16 a time when Satan was cast into that same area of hell.

> Everyone there [demons] will stare at you and ask, "Can this be the one [Satan] who shook the earth and the kingdoms of the world?" (NLT).

When God sent the demons to the pit, they lost all their rights to and authority on the earth. The only way a demon can get out of the pit is if someone calls them out. Humans release demons into the earth by calling them out directly or indirectly by occult practices. They roam the earth looking for someone to inhabit. They need an earthly body to inhabit to have an avenue to work through—someone they can express themselves through.

Nine Truths About Demons

As a foundation to our study on demons, let's look to the master himself, Jesus. In Matthew 12:43-45, Jesus provides us with nine truths about demons and how they operate:

> When the unclean spirit [another name for demon] is gone out of a man, he walketh through dry places, seeking rest, and findeth none. Then he saith, I will return into my house from whence I came out; and when he

is come, he findeth it empty, swept, and garnished. Then goeth he, and taketh with himself seven other spirits more wicked than himself, and they enter in and dwell there: and the last state of that man is worse than the first. Even so shall it be also unto this wicked generation.

1. *"walketh through dry places"* Demons are earth-bound and operate in the earthly realm. They are disembodied spirits seeking someone who will allow them to indwell.

2. Since this verse says they are walking, this also implies that they are able to travel.

3. *"seeking"* Implies intelligence in that they know how to seek and search for something. This also means they can see (vision) what they are searching for and yet not being able to find it. Demons must find a body to inhabit or they must go back to the pit. Remember, they have no right to live on the earth unless a man calls them out and offers up his body for their use.

4. *"seeking rest"* If a being seeks rest, then it can get tired and lose strength.

5. *"Then he saith"* Demons can speak.

6. *"I will"*—Implies a will and the ability to think and decide.

7. *"from whence I came out"* Demons can remember.

8. *"findeth it empty, swept, and garnished"* Shows the ability to investigate and examine.

9. *"Then goeth he, and taketh with himself seven other spirits"* Demons are able to plan and attack. It also shows that demons are able to work with each other to achieve the common goal.

These nine truths Jesus gave us show that demons were a highly intelligent race of beings, certainly capable of establishing governments and cities that Jeremiah 4:26 describes as being broken down after their fall with

Satan. So if they are capable of building cities, certainly they are persons with their own nature and way of being.

Nature of Demons
1. Are personal beings

In Luke 8:27-33 we find the story of a man who had been possessed by demons a long time. In verse 28, when the demons saw Jesus. They recognized him as the Son of God and asked him not to torment them. They also had the intellect, emotions, and will to make the request in verses 31 and 32. They asked Jesus that if they had to leave the man's body that he please not send them into the deep or the pit, but to send them into the pigs so that they would continue having something—even a pig's body—to inhabit and express themselves. Being the good Jewish man that he was (Jews of that day did not eat pork), Jesus obliged them. And just as with the men they inhabit, they destroyed the pigs. Demons want something or someone to inhabit to express themselves, but they always destroy them in the process.

2. Are spirit beings

Ephesians 6:12 says, "For we wrestle not against flesh and blood, but against principalities, against powers, against the rulers of the darkness of this world." Demons are spirit beings. They don't have a form of their own. They enter the form of others and use them as a vehicle of expression. So when you see someone acting like the devil, he may be possessed or being influenced by demons. God is never the author of evil.

In addition, Luke repeats the Matthew 12:43-45 event in Luke 11:24-25, which talks about the unclean spirit who is cast out of a man, leaves, comes back, finds him clean, goes and gets other demons, and in the end, the man is worse off. Here the demon calls the person his house. Demons need a house or body to reside in and express themselves. But a more important point is that once a person is set free, he had better not leave his house empty, thinking the demons won't come back. He had better invite Jesus into his heart and let the "greater one" fill him up.

3. Are powerful beings

Let it be known that demons are dangerous and powerful beings. Luke 8:29 describes how when they were in possession of a certain man's body, that man who had been bound with chains and shackles was able to break free and go into the dessert.

We also see this superhuman demonic strength and wildness in psychiatric conditions (although not all psychiatric conditions are demonic in nature), and in drug and alcohol users. This is because they are not just on drugs; the drug itself may be a demonic vehicle. Drugs, enchantments, sorcery, wizardry, and witchcraft are depicted in the Bible as vehicles that transport demonic activity (2 Chronicles 33:6). Most people think that it is just the materials in the marijuana leaf or in the drug that make you act crazy. This is not necessarily so. Some may be a vehicle guiding demons to their destination. I believe this can be seen in the large number of people who either use drugs to commit suicide or commit suicide while under the influence of a drug.

Revelation 9:3-6 seems to confirm this by showing us how demonic possession or activity can cause people to want to commit suicide as it describes how during the End Times demons or locust will be released from hell into the earth and will attack and sting men with the power to kill like scorpions. It goes on to say that they were told by God not to kill the people right away but to torment them for five months.

During those five months many will seek death but will not be able to find it. It's bad not to be able to find death and to be in the misery of it. As this verse shows, demons are powerful and dangerous beings, so much so that the Lord had to tell them explicitly, "You can torment them [people], but you can't kill them." I believe that the Lord held them back to give the men and women on the earth one last chance to repent of their sins and turn to God by accepting Jesus as the Lord of their life.

4. Are perverted beings

The *American Heritage Dictionary* defines *perverted* as one who is directed away from what is right and good, in error or fault, deviant, corrupt, debased, misuse, and one who incorrectly interprets truth. This definition correctly defines the character of demons. Because they chose to follow Satan and his evil angels, they turned away from God, who only is right and good. When they did this, they deviated from the truth through an error in judgment and turned from their good life with God. Ultimately, they made a mistake by interpreting Satan's smooth talk about his being more powerful than God, and they made an incorrect decision to follow Satan rather than God. When demons rejected God, they got their own name—devils, unclean or wicked spirits.

Doctrine of Demons

These evil spirits have the ability to influence even people of faith. Demons can't possess people of God, because God is in them. But if these people don't know the correct doctrines of the Christian faith, demons can deceive and influence their beliefs.

To influence people for evil, they operate under the "doctrine of demons." In this doctrine they pervert or reverse God's doctrine to encourage people to act the exact opposite of how God wants them to act and to convince people that God is not good or his creation is not good. As a Christian, you are to enjoy the things God gives you. This doctrine of demons is described in 1 Timothy 4:1-5:

The Spirit clearly says that in later times

some will abandon the faith and follow deceiving spirits and things taught by demons. Such teachings come through hypocritical liars, whose consciences have been seared with a hot iron. They forbid people to marry and order them to abstain from certain foods, which God created to be received with thanksgiving by those who believe and who know the truth. For everything God created is good, and nothing is to be rejected if it is received with thanksgiving, because it is consecrated by the word of God and prayer (NIV).

So the ultimate purpose of the doctrine of demons is that through deception they try to get you to turn away from God, and if they can't do that, they will try to slow you down in the accomplishment of God's plan and purpose for your life.

1. Undermine Jesus Christ

2 Corinthians 11:2-3 shows how it tries to distract from the worship, devotion, and simplicity of Jesus Christ. It puts satanic blinders on people so they can't see how they are saved by God's grace or mercy and not from their own works.

2. Promote Satan's plan of destruction

Often it is demonic forces at work debilitating people. All illness is not necessarily demonically orchestrated; however, they are doing a lot more than we give them credit for. In Matthew 12:22, they cause blindness and the inability to speak. In Matthew 9:32-33, a speechless man spoke after a demon was cast out. In Luke 13:11 they caused physical deformities. In Mark 5:1-10 demons caused a man to be a lunatic. Revelation 9:5 shows that they can cause physical death. Demons are responsible for many maladies. We must pray to find out the ultimate cause for our physical problems.

3. Promote Satan's domination

Revelation 16:14 provides a picture of how Satan wants to dominate the whole world. Daniel 10 shows how demons tried to block the archangel Gabriel from coming so that they could keep control of the political realm of Persia. As hard as it may be to believe, some political leaders and nations are controlled by demonic influence. These demon-influenced nations control their society to a degree that the people are not able to see and enjoy the blessings of God. Countries where witchcraft and sorcery flourish—such as Haiti and some parts of Africa—are often poor.

4. Promote Satan by distraction

Far too many Christians are dabbling in the spirit world, i.e. looking at the horoscope or playing with Ouija boards or tarot cards and are unaware of how demons are distracting them from Jesus Christ in their everyday life. Demons distract when they lure you away from total focus on God. To paraphrase, Leviticus 19:31 says no palm readers, no Ouija boards, and no crystal balls. To participate in these activities is to deny the existence of the living God who is in control of all things. Whenever you offer to the created what is the prerogative of the Creator, you change gods, as seen in Leviticus 20:6 where the people turned to mediums and harlots as the source of their supply.

5. Oppose God's position through idolatry

In Deuteronomy 32:17 the people sacrificed to demons, because behind every idol is a demon. An idol is anything that takes the place of God in your life, for example, money, person, house, car—anything operating as God in your life. In idol worship God must adjust to you rather than your adjusting to God. If that thing that has a central place in your life—what you worship and fellowship with—is not God, then you are dining with demons.

6. Want you to be impure

Demons want you to be impure, as opposed to possessing God's purity. We have learned how some of Satan's evil angels did not keep within their God-defined boundaries but left them and had sex with the women on the earth and as a result God chained them and sent them to a place to await their final judgment. Likewise, demons—their workhorses, influence men and women to be impure (Jude 4-7). They want you condemned to hell like they are.

7. Slander us before God

Evil angels and demons oppose us by slandering us before God. To them it is a technical victory, even though they know they are going to lose the war (Revelation 22). God is holy, so they report our sin to God so he can judge us. But if we accept Jesus as our Lord and Savior, he acts as our attorney based on the power of his blood that was shed on the cross in our behalf.

Remember that Jesus was a man, but he also is God. That was God on the cross dying for our sins and so our bodies could be healed (Isaiah 53:5). Romans 8:31-33 admonishes us with this, "Because God is for us, no one [including Satan and all his evil angels and demons] can be against us." God proved this by offering up his own Son on the cross for our sins and giving us eternal life in heaven with him if we accept his Son's sacrifice. Remember, it is Satan and his demons that are the "accusers of the brethren" (Revelation 12:10).

And these accusers can even influence the brethren. Going back to 1 Timothy 4, we see people teaching incorrectly on marriage, food, etc. This is not just bad teaching but is a doctrine from hell trying to seduce the people of the church to stray from the godly path. Again, as previously mentioned in the "Test the Angel" section of Chapter Two, it shows us how to know whether we are dealing with a doctrine of demons and what tests we can perform to diagnose these cases. So we test the spirit behind a doctrine by testing their response to Jesus Christ, and we look at 1 John 4:1-6 for a description of the test.

Demons . . .
1. Want to destroy us.
Peter informs us that Satan and his demons are like a lion looking for lunch. They want you!

> Be sober, be vigilant; because your adversary the devil, as a roaring lion, walketh about, seeking whom he may devour. (1 Peter 5:8)

2. Want to destroy your family.

> Let the husband render unto the wife due benevolence: and likewise also the wife unto the husband. The wife hath not power of her own body, but the husband: and likewise also the husband hath not power of his own body, but the wife. Defraud ye not one the other, except it be with consent for a time, that ye may give yourselves to fasting and prayer; and come together again, that Satan tempt you not for your incontinency. But I speak this by permission, and not of commandment. For I would that all men were even as I myself. But every man hath his proper gift of God, one after this manner, and another after that. I say therefore to the unmarried and widows, it is good for them if they abide even as I. But if they cannot contain, let them marry: for it is better to marry than to burn. (1 Corintians 7:3-9)

3. Want to destroy the church.
Ananias and Saphara were hurting the early church by lying. Demons used them to try to stop the church before it even got started.

> But a certain man named Ananias, with

121

Sapphira his wife, sold a possession, and kept back part of the price, his wife also being privy to it, and brought a certain part, and laid it at the apostles' feet. But Peter said, Ananias, why hath Satan filled thine heart to lie to the Holy Ghost, and to keep back part of the price of the land? While it remained, was it not thine own? And after it was sold, was it not in thine own power? Why hast thou conceived this thing in thine heart? Thou hast not lied unto men, but unto God. And Ananias hearing these words fell down, and gave up the ghost, and great fear came on all them that heard these things (Acts 5:1-4).

4. Seek to destroy communities.

Demons seek to destroy communities by turning people away from these basic rules on how to treat one another:

Children, obey your parents in the Lord: for this is right. Honor thy father and mother; (which is the first commandment with promise) That it may be well with thee, and thou mayest live long on the earth. And, ye fathers, provoke not your children to wrath: but bring them up in the nurture and admonition of the Lord.

Servants, be obedient to them that are your masters according to the flesh, with fear and trembling, in singleness of your heart, as unto Christ; Not with eye service, as men pleasers; but as the servants of Christ, doing the will of God from the heart; with good will doing service, as to the Lord, and not to men: Knowing that whatsoever good thing any man doeth, the same shall he receive of the Lord, whether he be bond or free. And, ye

> masters, do the same things unto them, forbearing threatening: knowing that your Master also is in heaven; neither is there respect of persons with him. (Ephesians 6:1-9).

5. Seek to destroy societies and nations.

Some geopolitical realms are demonized and controlled by evil angels.

> But the prince of the kingdom of Persia withstood me one and twenty days: but, lo, Michael, one of the chief princes, came to help me; and I remained there with the kings of Persia (Daniel 10:13).

Many demons dwell in Babylon, which is in the area of modern day Iraq.

> And after these things I saw another angel come down from heaven, having great power; and the earth was lightened with his glory. And he cried mightily with a strong voice, saying, Babylon the great is fallen, is fallen, and is become the habitation of devils, and the hold of every foul spirit, and a cage of every unclean and hateful bird (Revelation 18:1-2).

Protection from demonic activity in your life and home

1. Give no place to the devil

Ephesians 4:27 admonishes us to give no place to the devil. This seems to say if you don't give the devil a place in your life by doing evil things, things that are of his nature, than he can't have access to or take part in your life. Luke 10:19 seems to confirm this when it promises that no demon can harm you. But there is a condition to this that can be found in Psalm 91:13, which says we shall trample on the dragon, serpents, lion, or any other demonic condition as we dwell in the secret place of the

Most High and dwell in the shadow of the Almighty.

If you stay in God's presence and in his will, then you're safe, because the evil one has to come through God himself to get to you and he can't do that. On the other hand, if you stray, you are in trouble (Malachi 4:3). Never walk in the devil's territory. Never go unless God says go. If you go on your own, don't expect the Lord to protect you. Only if you dwell with the Most High God will you be safe.

This promise only works, however, in a life of obedience to God. You can't claim this promise of protection and live in rebellion. God reminds us in Leviticus 19:19 that there is to be no mixing of the godly things with the ungodly, because it opens you to demonic activity. "This is truth, and the truth you know will set and keep you free" (John 8:36).

2. Ephesians 6: Seven steps to God's protection

There are seven things that we as believers can do to keep ourselves safe. Look at Ephesians 6 to see how to keep safe. In a nutshell it tells us to recognize that we are not fighting against flesh and blood or people but powerful evil spirits. Then we are to be strong in the Lord. Next we are to put on the armor of God. Ephesians 6:14-17 gives us six specific pieces of armor including the belt of truth, the breastplate of righteousness, shoes of peace, the shield of faith, the helmet of salvation, and lastly, our weapon, the sword of the Spirit, which is the word of God.

1. Verse 13 commands us to put on the armor of God. This verse says specifically that if we don't, then we won't be able to stand against the attacks of the enemy. Some people automatically state that any tragedy is an act of God and often comment about "how could God let this happen?" This is not a true accusation. Jesus says in John 10:10, "The thief cometh not but for to steal, kill, and destroy, but I have come to give you life and give it more abundantly." Just as there is a good God, there is a mean devil who's out to kill you, steal from you, and destroy you, and the only way to protect yourself is by the power of God. God gives us the armor, but we have to put it on.

2. Verse 14 instructs us to gird (to undergird or support) our loins with the truth and to have on our breastplate of righteousness. "Loins" deals with the mind. 1 Peter 1:13 advises us to gird up the loins of our mind. So the first job in protecting ourselves is to get the word of God in our mind. So to tighten the belt of truth around our loins is to hold tightly to the word of God and allow it to transform our minds to think in line with God's word. We do this by daily spending time reading the Bible and praying.

The door to the spirit is the mind. If you protect your mind, you are automatically protecting your spirit and body. So learn the Scriptures and let them transform your mind or thinking into God's way of thinking and doing. If you think and act like God, then no devil in hell can stand against you. You need to transform and renew your mind because the mind is the door to the spirit. It opens into your heart or spirit, which is the very essence of who a person is.

The breastplate covers and protects your spirit. Wearing the breastplate of righteousness means having a deep understanding of who we are in Christ—knowing that we are children of God and that we've been made righteous through faith in what Jesus did, not what we do.

Since mankind's fall in the Garden of Eden, humanity was separated from God by sin. God says in the Bible that the only way a man's spirit can be cleansed of sin and reunited (made righteous or gain right standing) with God is by the shedding of blood. Through the shedding of Jesus' blood on the cross, God cleansed us of sin and restored our right relation or right standing with himself. We must keep this breastplate of righteousness on at all times, and we do this by always remembering the price God paid to bring us close to him—so that we live in his presence—safe from all harm.

It's like the little kid standing behind his father holding on to his shirttail as an angry neighbor yells at the child for breaking his window. The son says, "I'm sorry," but the man keeps yelling. Finally the father says, "Leave him alone; my older son will pay the price for his sin." The little child knows now that he is safe, that his father and older brother have forgiven him and will keep him safe from the neighbor's wrath. When you have a deep understanding of your victory accomplished by Jesus on the cross, it protects you from demonic influence.

3. Verse 15 admonishes us to keep our feet shod or covered with gospel of peace. Putting on the shoes of peace means that we strive to walk in peace with ourselves, with God and with others. We can do this by allowing the word of God to affect our walk or behavior in life. The word of God should go into your mind, into your spirit and then come out in your behavior. If you consistently express godly behavior, then you are dwelling with or living in the manner God wants you to live, and you will be protected. Are you loving, courteous, giving, helpful? If so, you are protected.

4. Verse 16 commands us to take the shield of faith to quench or stop all the fiery darts (attacks) of the wicked. The shield of faith represents an ongoing state of believing and trusting God's promises instead of believing in ourselves, our circumstances, or what others say. Romans 10:17 says that faith comes by hearing the word of God. So our response to attacks by the enemy should be directed by what God says our response should be. For example, if you feel an unusual symptom in your body, the Bible doesn't tell you to deny the symptom or disease. It tells us to:

> Speak to the mountain (sickness is a mountain in the way of your comfort) and tell it to be removed and it shall go (Matthew 21:21; Mark 11:23).

> The believer (in Jesus Christ as Savior and Lord) shall lay hands on the sick and they shall recover (Mark 16:18).

> With Jesus' stripes you were healed (Isaiah 53:5 and 1 Peter 2:24).

So if you pray in faith and tell (speak with your mouth) that mountain of sickness to leave your body, if you lay hands on your body and command it to be recovered, and believe that Jesus' stripes saved your soul and healed your body, you will be healed. Whether instantly or over a period of time, it will happen.

When you put up your shield of faith or belief in God's word as the ultimate truth and not in the fiery dart's ability to harm you, the fiery dart will go Sssssssss and go out as quickly as it appeared. So lift up the shield of faith and it will protect you against every fiery dart that comes your way.

5. Verse 17 tells us to take the helmet of salvation and the sword of the Spirit. The helmet of salvation mentioned here is not only talking about the mind; it deals with doctrine and balance. First, the helmet of salvation protects our thinking. It is a clear understanding of what it means to be saved based on God's word. Secondly, it deals with doctrine and balance. It is being in one mind, heart, walk, and actions with God, so much so that it becomes your nature.

So the helmet spoken of here deals with correct thinking and what we believe. The doctrine of the word of

God makes us who we are. "I'm stable, not moved by error, taken by false teaching, not following every new thing that comes along, because I base my life on the Bible or God's word." Unbalanced people are too weak to lift up the sword of the Spirit and are easily defeated. The helmet of salvation brings balance and strength to our life, and you will not be broken but will have victory in every area of your life.

All of the other protections in Ephesians 6 are defensive; the "sword of the Spirit which is the word of God" is the only one mentioned here as offensive. As we hide the word of God in our hearts, we give the Holy Spirit the ammunition he needs to recall to our memory the specific scripture that will cut away and destroy Satan's attack.

Also, the word of God brings movement to your life. It compels you to act, to go forward and take back old and new territory. When you wield the sword of the word of God by speaking it out of your mouth in faith, the devil doesn't see you. He sees God and obeys the word and quickly backpedals out of your life.

6. *Verse 18 directs us to pray always.* Prayer is the catalyst that energizes and empowers the armor of God, releasing God's wisdom and power into every situation we face. When we pray, it covers us like a supernatural mantle and the enemy can't get through it to harm us.

7. Although this is not in Ephesians 6, *it is important that we not allow certain things in our houses.* Just as demons can inhabit a person's body, they can inhabit a thing. Don't allow items associated with the occult, Buddha, good luck charms or if you come across an item while traveling that might seem like a perfect souvenir, but you don't know what it is or what's printed on it— don't bring it into your house, no matter how harmless it may seem. If you do, you may unknowingly open your front door and allow a demon to freely walk into your house.

The difference between demons and evil angels
1. The Bible documents them as different

The Bible does not document evil angels and demons as being the same creature, but addresses them as two separate beings—calling angels, angels and demons, demons.

Specifically, this differentiation is seen in Romans 8:38 of the New International Version and in the New Living Translation, during the discussion of who or what can separate us from the love of God. "Neither death, nor life, nor angels, nor demons . . . can separate us from the love of God." If they were not two entirely different species, why would they be listed as such? It would be tantamount to a listing of dogs, cats, humans, and birds. Looking at this list, one would assume—and rightly so— that they are of a different species.

2. They live in different places

In addition to this, the Bible speaks of evil angels as heaven-bound (the second heaven) and demons as earthbound or in the pit (Revelation 9:1 and 12:7; Ephesians 6; Matthew 12:43-45).

3. Demons need rest and angels don't

Another major difference between demons and angels is that the Bible says angels don't need rest (Revelation 4:8), but demons can grow tired and seek rest (Matthew 12:43).

4. Angels can manifest themselves in their own body, but demons cannot

Angels also differ from demons in that angels can manifest themselves in a body (Judges 13:6 and Acts 1:10), but demons cannot manifest themselves in their own body (Mark 5:1-13). In addition, the Bible never talks about how a demon looks except in Revelation 9, which describes them as they are being released from hell in the End Times. The Bible only talks about them possessing another person's body. This is because as a part of the pre-Adamic race, they no longer have any authority on the earth except that a man or woman gives it to them by giving up their body for their use. Demons need to inhabit a person's body to operate through, and they will search about looking for one (Matthew 12:43-45 and Luke 8:31).

The opposing view: Demons and angels are the same beings

Pastor, preacher, and teacher Tony Evans in his tape series, "Angels: The Good, Bad, and Ugly," presents the more popular view, describing good angels as God's angels, bad angels are the fallen or demonic angels, and the ugly angel is Satan himself. He groups the fallen angels and demons in the same category. He makes no differentiation in the two beings and seems to use the two terms "bad angels" and "demons" interchangeably. He does not address their origins separately. He does mention however, that differences may occur in levels of authority and power.

Although this is a popular view, it is unscriptural, because as we have seen, the Bible never lumps demons and angels in the same category but speaks of them always as two distinct beings, as well as presenting multiple differences in evil angels and demons.

Concluding Thought

Even though others may disagree, I believe
- the Bible addresses evil angels and demons as different beings
- they live in different places,
- one can manifest himself in his own body and the other cannot, and

· one needs rest and the other doesn't.

Thus, chances are they are two different entities. As the old saying goes with just a little twist, if it doesn't look like a duck and doesn't quack like a duck, then it must not be a duck.

CHAPTER SEVEN

Angels in End Time Prophecy

Increased activity of angels

Jerry Savelle, noted speaker and minister of the gospel feels that toward the end of this age, right before the second return of Jesus Christ, there will be an increase in the activity of angels. In his 2001 teaching tape called "Increased Activity of Angels," Savello said that it is God's plan and purpose to make known to his children his secrets as well as his plan and purpose for their lives (Ephesians 1:7-9).

He feels that the apostle Paul was seeing something in the Spirit about the last-day church—us—when Paul was talking about the ages to come in Ephesians 2:7. God decided before the beginning of time (verses 8-9) to tell us his plans for our life, and this scripture goes on to say that he keeps them ready for those who love him. 1 Corinthians 2:9 carries this a step further when the apostle Paul explains that our "eyes have not seen, nor our ears heard the plans God has made and keeps ready for those who love him."

So how do we lay our hands on the things God has planned for us in the right here and now? Savelle feels it is by looking at God, our example. How does God get his desired results? He speaks the thing into existence and declares the end of a thing from the beginning (Isaiah 46:10). So, according to Isaiah, it seems as if God speaks it and brings it to pass. Mankind is created in the image of God, including the God-like ability to speak a thing in faith (in line with the words of the Bible) and have his desire come to pass. So what does this have to do with angels?

Savelle says:

> In the past we have taken too lightly the part of angels play in all of this. We're not doing this alone. We're not just speaking authoritatively the word of God. The angels have an assignment to take those words and make them come to pass.

Psalm 103:20 seems to agree with Savelle when it discusses how God's angels harken to, respond to, pay attention to, carry out his words, and do his commandments. To harken means to attend to what has been uttered. To give heed to and obey, to comply to, and to perform or execute what has been uttered. When God releases a commandment, the angels work with his words to bring the thing to pass

Savelle feels that if that's the way it works with God, and if we have the same spirit of faith, that means when we utter or speak the word of God with our voice, the angels pay attention to it and carry out God's word spoken out of our mouths concerning a thing. The problem in the past is that the angels had not been hearing anything that they could respond to coming out of our mouths.

Angels don't hearken to unbelief, complaining, or speaking the problem. They only pay attention to and carry out God's word spoken in faith over a situation. Savelle says that when a believer, a child of God who has the divine nature of God, speaks God's words, the angels hear it, and when they hear it, they know they're under assignment by God. They don't question it; they don't have the right to decide whether they will obey it or not. They are under charge or assignment by God to hearken, comply, perform, and execute that word.

Angels are obligated to perform God's word spoken in faith. They have no choice. The only angels not obligated to obey have already been kicked out of heaven. All the rest obey. So that great innumerable host that is left, that are far greater than Satan's gang, are obligated, on assignment, to perform whatever comes out of the mouth of God or the one who possesses his nature, born again of his Spirit. In the eyes of God your words carry the same authority as his words because your words are his words.

Joel 2:11 confirms this when it describes how God's army powerfully executes God's word. Joel isn't talking about men; he's talking about angels.

Jerry Savelle's teaching is also in line with Hebrews 1:14 which essentially says that angels are servants sent out in the service of God for the assistance of those who are to inherit salvation. So when God utters his word and when we utter his word, angels are not just God's servants, they are our servants as well. They are assigned to the service of God and to the assistance of those inheriting salvation—you and me. The angels are servants of God doing God's service in our behalf. They are assigned to us, and when we speak God's word, they are obligated to perform and execute whatever we say when we're saying God's word.

Angels are commanded by God to execute his word when it comes out of his mouth or out of our mouth. They are required to do his pleasure, "Ye ministers of his that do his pleasure" (Psalm 103:20-21).

If God has gone to the trouble of creating paths before the foundation of the earth that you and I might live the good life, don't you suppose he would get his angels involved? Psalm 35:27 reminds us that "the Lord has pleasure in prosperity of his servant." So if we say the word that the Lord has pleasure in the prosperity of me, his servant, what do you suppose the angels will be doing? They will be helping us to prosper. We say it continually so the angels will hearken.

Psalm 103:20 says that angels excel in strength or get stronger as they carry out God's word. They get stronger and stronger the more you say it. This is an important point because there is resistance by Satan out there. There are principalities and powers trying to stop them from carrying out God's word, but the more you say God's word, the stronger they get. It appears they feed on the word of God, or in other words, hearing the word of God is the breakfast of angels. As people learn how to correctly stimulate the activity of angels in their lives, we will see more and more evidences of angelic presence on the earth.

Along this same line of thought, Savelle mentions in his "Increased Activities of Angels" tape that the late Christian minister, William Branham, prophesied that there would come a time before the return of Jesus that God's people would speak a thing and it would happen instantly. The only way we can speak a thing and have it happen immediately is for God to accelerate the activity of angels because they are the ones who hearken to the word, perform it, and execute it.

We're going to see increased angelic activity before the return of Jesus, because it will take them, as we are speaking, to make it come to pass instantly. Therefore, we will have accelerated angelic activity. The Bible says that Satan plans to intensify the activity of his spirits as the end of this age approaches, so it makes sense that God would intensify the activity of his angels. God won't let the devil get the upper hand.

In 2 Peter 2:3 and in Jude 6 the Scriptures reveal to us that there are evil angels and demon spirits who have been reserved for the last days. Their assignment has been withheld until the last days and, if possible, they will deceive even the elect of God (Matthew 24:24). They will even be able to transform themselves into angels of light (2 Corinthians 11:14), and if you are not well established in the word of God, you will be deceived. Again, if Satan plans to intensify the activity of his evil angels and demons, it's not unreasonable to say that God will intensify the activity of his angels.

In fact, the great harvest of souls God is planning at the end of this age, will be reaped by the angels (Matthew 13:39). God is planning a harvest of souls like no other generation has seen, so there will have to be increased activity of the angels to bring that harvest in. I believe we will see whole nations be saved and angels will harvest or set the stage for people to accept Jesus as their Savior. This gang of people will come in due to accelerated angel activity.

We need to become more aware of the activity of angels in our lives today. The activity of angels was not uncommon in the New Testament church. I believe that as more people are made aware of how to activate the angels by speaking God's word, the more activity we will see.

The angels are waiting to hear God's word come out of our mouth so they can execute it on our behalf. Stop talking the circumstance. Start talking God's word concerning your situation. When God summons a thing, that thing now has a divine appointment with God. When we call, speak, or summon something based on God's word in the Bible, that thing now has an appointment with us. Create a divine appointment for you and the thing that God has kept ready for you by calling them into the now and expecting the angels to execute the words that came from your mouth. Don't give up. Be consistent and begin to watch for accelerated manifestations, and don't be surprised when it happens, because this is the last day. A sample prayer might go like this:

> Father, I come to you in the name of Jesus, asking you to protect me and my family. According to Psalm 91 we live continuously in the presence of the Most High God. You, O God, are our refuge, our fortress, our protection. You promised, Lord, that you would deliver us from the evil one's snare and disease and pestilence. You promised that you would cover me and my family and be a shield to us. We will not fear terrorists by day or night. A thousand people shall fall by our side, ten thousand at our right hand, but it will not come near us. No evil or atomic bombs shall befall us. Neither shall any plague or biological warfare germs come near our dwelling, because we trust you, Lord, that you have put your angels in charge of protecting us and keeping us in all our comings and goings. I thank you, Father, that I know your name and you know mine and that when I call unto you, you will answer me and deliver me and honor me. With long life will you satisfy me and show me your complete salvation. I give you all the honor and praise, in Jesus' name. Amen.

I think John Calvin summed it up speaking on the ministry of angels when he said in his *Institutes of the Christian Religion, I*: "The angels are the dispensers and administrators of the divine beneficence [Bible benefits] toward us. They regard our safety, undertake our defense, direct our ways, and exercise a constant solicitude that no evil befalls us."

Three angelic messages of Revelation 14:6-14

God's present truth for today is contained in the

three angelic messages of Revelation 14. Of course, salvation through Jesus Christ alone is central to these messages. However, the "present truth" of the three angels also has been given to prepare people for Jesus' second coming and to open their eyes to Satan's highly convincing deceptions. Unless people understand these messages, Satan will indeed capture and destroy them. Jesus knew we needed these three special messages, so in loving kindness he has given them.

The Foundation: The two crucial points of Revelation 14:6

Before we go into the discussion of the three angel messages, it is important to set the foundation for it.

> And I saw another angel fly in the midst of heaven having the everlasting gospel to preach unto them that dwell on the earth, and to every nation, and kindred, and tongue, and people. (Revelation 14:6)

The two crucial points are that 1) there is an everlasting gospel, and 2) it must be preached to every person on the earth. This verse sets the stage for the three angels' messages which stress the gospel—that people are saved by faith in and acceptance of Jesus Christ alone (Acts 4:12). Since God said in the Bible that this Jesus is the way to salvation, then it is evil to claim that there is some other way.

Satan's counterfeit ways to salvation are two very effective ones: salvation by works and salvation in sin. The first, salvation by works, says I can be saved and go to heaven by my own good deeds. Salvation with sin says I can purposefully continue to sin and still go to heaven. Both are saying that Jesus, the Savior, is not necessary, which is in direct opposition to what the Bible says, that salvation is through Jesus Christ alone.

Without realizing it, many have embraced one of

these two errors and are trying to build their salvation upon it, which is an utterly impossible feat. Anyone preaching the gospel of Jesus Christ during this End Time will always include the three angelic messages.

First angelic message

> Saying with a loud voice, "Fear God, and give glory to him; for the hour of his judgment is come: and worship him that made heaven, and earth, and the sea, and the fountains of water" (Revelation 14:7).

Fear God. This means we should respect God and look upon him with love and trust, eager to do his bidding. We are not speaking of fear as in "afraid," but in a reverent way. This keeps us from evil. "By the fear of the Lord men depart from evil" (Proverbs 16:6).

Give glory to God. We fulfill this command when we obey, praise, and thank God for his goodness to us. One of the major sins of the last days is that people are not thankful for the good things God has given them (2 Timothy 3:1-2).

The hour of judgment is come. This indicates that everyone is accountable to God, and it is a clear statement that the judgment is now in session. I like the way the Living Bible says this because it leaves no doubt as to who is judging when it says, "Fear God . . . for the time has come when he will sit as judge." We will all be judged by God, the saints for the timeframe since their conversion to Christianity and sinners for every sin they ever committed.

Worship the Creator. All this means is just to tell God how much you love and respect him for who he is. This command is to reject idolatry of all kinds, including self-worship. The overstressing of self-worth leads to self-worship. A Christian's self-worth is in Jesus the Christ, who makes us sons and daughters of the King of heaven. This portion of Scripture also totally repudiates evolution, which denies that God is Creator and Redeemer. Our true roots are found in God alone, who made us in his image in the beginning. Those who do not worship God as Creator—no matter what else they may worship—may never discover their real roots.

Second angelic message

> And there followed another angel, saying, Babylon is fallen (Revelation 14:8).

> I saw another angel come down from heaven . . . And he cried mightily with a strong voice, saying, Babylon the great is fallen . . . And I heard another voice from heaven, saying, Come out of her my people (Revelation 18:1-4).

The second angel solemnly states that "Babylon is fallen," and the voice from heaven urges all of God's people to come out of Babylon at once. Babylon here is symbolic of the antichrist—the one against Jesus Christ—or the Satan-controlled world. On the surface the evil-dominated world can look good, and unless believers understand who is behind it, they could be tempted to participate in its delicacies.

Third angelic message

> And the third angel followed them, saying with a loud voice: If any man worships the beast and his image, and receives his mark in his forehead, or in his hand, the same shall drink of the wine of the wrath of God (Revelation 14:9-10).

The third angelic message solemnly warns people not to worship the beast, his image, or to receive the mark of the beast on their foreheads or hands. The first angel commands the true worship of God. The third angel tells of the awesome consequences of the false worship of Satan.

In case you haven't already guessed, the beast is the

antichrist—or one against Jesus Christ—Satan. The mark of the beast I believe is quite possible now, because we have the technology to implant a computer chip in a person's hand or forehead that would allow Satan's men to tell at a swipe of a scanning wand who belongs to the beast and who does not. Concerning the worshiping an image—this is also possible now with computerized imagery and virtual reality. It is possible for Satan to project an artificial image of himself for people to worship. He would never show his true image because all people, even people who don't know God, would be repelled by it.

Description of those who accept and obey the three angelic messages

> Here is the patience of the saints: here are
> they that keep the commandments of God,
> and the faith of Jesus (Revelation 14:12).

They are patient, persevering, and faithful to the end. This is a big order for the do-it-now, microwave generation we live in. God's people reveal him by their patient, loving conduct.

They are saints. They are holy ones because they are fully on God's side.

They keep the commandments of God. These people of God joyfully obey his commandments given to them. Their first aim is to please God whom they love (1 John 3:22).

They have the faith of Jesus. This could also be translated "faith in Jesus." In either case, God's people fully follow Jesus and fully trust him.

What happens immediately after the three angelic messages?

> And I looked, and behold a white cloud, and
> upon the cloud one sat like the Son of man,

141

having on his head a gold crown (Revelation 14:14).

Immediately after the three angelic messages are spoken to every person, Jesus returns in the clouds (his second coming) to take his people to their heavenly home.

CHAPTER EIGHT

Angels With Us in Heaven

HEAVEN

Now that it's over
There's no more use for guns and war
Cost me a lifetime
Just to gain this life's reward

They say streets of gold
Can you imagine somewhere
Where life will never end
No one ever grows old
Oh, my brother, please
Come with me

It's what I live for
A place where love will never cease
Willing to die for
Heaven is where I want to be

There are instructions
We must follow to a tee
In order to reach there
And there is where I want to be

143

No more nights
There is a place
Where there'll be no more crying
He is the light
Counting those days
When we meet in that place

BeBe & CeCe Winans

1988 BeBe & CeCe Winans HEAVEN album,
Yellow Elephant Music, Inc./Class Reunion Music/Benny's
Music/Dasnice Music (ASCAP/BMI),
1996 BeBe & CeCe Winans Greatest Hits,
EMI Records/The Sparrow Corporation.

The more heavenly minded I become, the more convinced I am of the presence of angels. The best part of heaven may be getting to know and fellowship with the angels. They love God and enjoy us. I can imagine that many angels have been surprised at our ways and snicker at our jokes.

Speaking of snickering, in a book written in 1994 by comedian and evangelist Jessie Duplantis, *Close Encounters of the God Kind,* he describes how in August 1988 he was taken to heaven by the angels and had an encounter with the Lord. While there, Jesus showed him around heaven, introducing him to many people and angels, including the apostle Paul, who was still calling Matthew, Mark, Luke, and John "my gospel."

Jesus even took him to the throne of God the Father. Duplantis said that the glory around the throne was so great he kept falling down, as well as the angels worshiping him. "I never did see his face. I could only lift my head high enough to see his feet. Ha, ha, truth," said Duplantis. He also said that the streets really are made of gold. He also found that the Lord had assigned children to teach immature adult Christians about the things of God. "Now I think that's really funny—kids teaching adults, but that's because they have greater faith," said Duplantis.

Taking advantage of the situation, Duplantis said he asked the Lord many questions while he was in heaven, and the Lord answered them all. One memorable question he mentions is that he asked, "I've seen you and I've seen the Father, but where is the Holy Spirit?" Jesus smiled. Duplantis said, "Oops, that's right, I forgot, he's on the earth, isn't he?"

After the question about the Spirit, Duplantis asked Jesus one last question, "Lord, why did you bring me here to heaven?" Jesus answered, "I brought you here to tell you, go tell them I'm coming, I'm coming soon!" After this, Duplantis said, he was then flown back to earth by another angel.

In the next story, "Life in Heaven," an eleven-year-old girl named Marygold, describes what a young Christian woman may have experienced upon her entrance into heaven and what she feels life in heaven will be like in a way that's far beyond her years. Here's her story.

Life in Heaven

She saw a bright light. Brighter than she had ever seen. She was a woman named Lana. Lana was a Christian. She had been in a car crash and was very badly hurt. She had a concussion. Lana was 25 years old. All of a sudden she closed her eyes and breathed her last breath. All her pain was gone and when the light shone upon her she floated up in the air.

She looked down at the ground and saw her husband, mother, father, and brother crowded around her, all crying. Lana wanted to say goodbye to them before she left. She wanted to reach out to them and to hold them in her arms. She knew she could only watch. She was going to see the Lord of lords, the King of kings. She was going to see Jesus. She knew she would see her family again. When they died, she would see them if they had Christ in their hearts still. She knew that they would go to heaven because they were totally obsessed with Jesus.

As she was looking at her family, she heard a voice. "Come, live in my light of peace and happiness, where everything is glorious and safe. Nothing can harm you now, my child." She knew it was Jesus. She looked at the light and was then walking towards it. As she walked up, her hospital clothes turned to white, soft, shining garments and made her look like a princess. Then, as she stopped to look at her clothes, a golden light appeared all around her head. She started walking again with a broad smile on her face.

She passed the light, and before she knew it, she was at the doorway to heaven. She walked up to the gates, and they opened. Lana felt so happy! She heard the most beautiful music she had ever heard, and she started to dance. She was laughing and giggling when others started to join the fun. She was soon crowded with a big welcoming. She said hello to all the angels and people, and started to walk towards the King's palace.

She entered the palace and saw him, The Creator of all things! She saw Jesus. "Welcome to heaven, my child," Jesus said to her and touched her face. His hands felt as if they were made of sheep wool, so soft and gentle against her cheek.

She touched his hands and looked at his palm. She saw the holes from his crucifixion. "Thank you," Lana said. Jesus knew what she meant. She said thank you for dying for our sins.

Jesus seems to agree with Marygold's story when he told in Luke 15:10 a parable about sinners gaining entrance into the kingdom of heaven, "I tell you, there is rejoicing in the presence of the angels of God over one sinner who repents." If angels rejoice so happily over our conversion, then you know they will cheer mightily upon our arrival at the foot of the throne of God, because they will have seen our redemption completed from beginning with mankind's fall in the Garden of Eden to the end with our triumphant entrance into heaven.

Angels Will Worship with Us

As citizens of heaven, we will also worship God with the angels. They've had a lot of practice at worshiping, as well as access to heaven's throne. They've seen it all. Yet when we arrive in heaven, it will be their privilege to worship with us. Just think of what it will be like: the crowd, the noise, the praise! Revelation 5:11-13 gives us a picture of what we might see:

> Then I looked and heard the voice of many angels, numbering thousands upon thousands, and ten thousand times ten thousand... In a loud voice they sang: "Worthy is the Lamb, who was slain, to receive power and wealth and wisdom and strength and honor and glory and praise!"

It reminds me of the time I was at a Benny Hinn crusade at the Fort Worth, Texas Convention Center. There was what seemed like about 10,000 people, all singing and praising the Lord. The heaviness of God's anointing came into that convention center so much so that I was having trouble standing up. I was surrounded by the sound of pure worship. It was powerful, clear and deep, enveloping me, resonating through my bones, and seemingly vibrating the arena. I tried to continue singing, but I couldn't get a note out, I was laughing, crying, hands held high—a moment of ecstasy so God-anointed that I believe that I was carried heavenward. All I could do was enjoy the ride. So, if an earthly choir of human voices and music could move me so much, how much more when our voices of praise and worship are combined with the angels in heaven.

Serve Us

Hebrews 1:14 describes angels as "ministering spirits, sent forth to minister for them who shall be heirs of
salvation," but I believe that this job description extends
beyond serving us while we're on earth. Angels will also
serve us in heaven. It is said in Romans 5:17 that we will
rule and reign with Christ Jesus. Well, Jesus is in
heaven. We will reign with Jesus; and he has been given
authority over all the heavenly hosts, so we will reign
over angels also. Will we rule over a few or a legion?
What will we command them to do? No one knows for
sure, but we can imagine. Even if we don't have leadership skills on earth, remember, when we get to heaven,
we will have glorified and perfect minds, so we will be
able to easily command the angels and lead the way in
doing God's work in heaven, as well as on earth.

Judged by Us

When it comes to fallen angels—all those who have
sworn allegiance to Satan—we will judge them all, including Satan himself. 1 Corinthians 6:3 spells this out in
black and white when it says, "Know ye not that we shall
judge angels?" Isn't this incredible that the Lord would
allow us to judge the very ones who have wreaked havoc
on mankind since the days in the Garden of Eden? I call
it righteous revenge!

When I see pictures of the Nazi holocaust, the
bombed out buildings in Oklahoma City, and the video
clips of the planes crashing into the World Trade Center
on 9/11, I don't blame God. I know who is ultimately
behind this evil—the devil. One day while carrying out
justice on the fallen angels, I will have the pleasure of
demonstrating "perfect hatred," as Psalm 139:22 puts it,
against "the powers, principalities, and the rulers of
darkness" (Ephesians 6:12).

Yes, being with the angels in heaven will be a glorious thing. We will be with the God of wonders, who is far beyond this galaxy. We will be holy like him. We will help to declare his majesty to the entire universe. The Lord of heaven and earth and angels and men will declare his victory both now and forever more.

Works Consulted

A Book of Angels. Sophy Burnham. New York, Ballantine Press, 1990.

A Gathering of Angels. Rabbi Morris B. Marigolie. New York, NY, Ballantine, 1994.

American Heritage Dictionary, Third Edition. New York, NY, Bantam, Double Day, Dell Publishing Group, 1994.

An Angel Called My Name . . . L.A. Justice. New York, NY, American Media Inc., 2001.

An Angel Is . . . Arlene B. Nickerson. Kansas City, MO, Andrews and McMeel, 1995.

An Angel's Story. Max Lucado. Nashville, TN, Word Publishing, 2002.

And the Angels Were Silent. Max Lucado. Sisters, OR, Multnomah Publishers, 1992

Angels. Armand Eisen. Kansas City, MO, Universal Press Syndicate Co., 1993.

Angels. Kenneth L. Woodward. *Newsweek,* December 27, 1993.

Angels, God's Secret Agents. Billy Graham. Nashville, TN, Thomas Nelson Publishers, 1994.

Angels, Good, Bad, & Ugly Audiotape Series. Anthony T. Evans. Dallas, TX, The Urban Alternative Ministries, 2002.

Angels In Our Midst. Liesl Vazquez. White Plains, NY, Peter Pauper Press Inc, 1996.

Angels' Instruction Book. Eileen E. Freeman. New York, NY, Warner Books, 1994.

Angels On The Earth Magazine. A division of Guidepost. New York, NY.

Angels On Your Side. Kenneth Copeland. Fort Worth, TX, *Believer's Voice of Victory Magazine*, September 2001.

Angels, The Mysterious Messengers Video tape. Alexandria, VA, Greystone Communications/American Artists Film Corp., Time Life Video, 1994.

Angels Videotape Series. Gloria Copeland. Fort Worth, TX, Believers Voice of Victory Television Broadcast, July 18, 2003.

BeBe & CeCe Greatest Hits: Heaven Recording , BeBe & CeCe Winans. New York,NY. EMI/Sparrow Records, 1996.

Encyclopedia of Angels. Constance V. Briggs. New York, NY, The Penguin Group, 1997.

Hugs from Heaven, On Angel Wings. G.A. Myers. West Monroe, LA, Howard Publishing Company, 1998.

Illustrated Encyclopedia of Bible Facts. J Packer, Merrill Tenney, William White. Nashville, TN. Thomas Nelson Publishers, 1995.

Increased Activity of Angels Audio tape. Jerry Savalle. Crowley, TX, Jerry Savalle Ministries, 2001.

Matthew Henry's Concise Commentary of the Bible. Quick Verse Computer Program; Version 7, Omaha, NE, The Parsons Church Group, 2000.

Somewhere Angels, Larry Libby. Nashville, TN. Thomas Nelson Publishers, 1990.

Straight Ahead: Angels Recording, Amy Grant. Waco, TX, Myrrh Records, 1984.

Strong's Exhaustive Concordance with Dictionaries of Hebrew and Greek Words. James H. Strong. Grand Rapids, MI, Baker Book House, 1989.

The Pursuit of God, A.W. Tozer. Christian Publications, 1948.

War in the Heavenlies Audio tape Series. Benny Hinn. Orlando, FL, Benny Hinn Ministries, 2000.

Zondervan Pictorial Encyclopedia of the Bible. Grand Rapids, MI, Zondervan Publishers, 1998.

The Author

Gloria Harris calls herself a "minister of writing." Her goal is to "write the vision and make it plain." (Habakkuk 2:2).

Reverend Harris is an angel of mercy (registered nurse), who also has an M.A. in theology-Christian education from Oral Roberts University and an M.A. in journalism-mass communication from the University of Oklahoma. In addition, Harris has served in the past as internet pastor and webmaster for six years for the Christian Info Net; A Technoministry of the Gospel of Christ website, held the position of staff writer for the Tulsa Christian Times newspaper, authored articles for the Christian Journal of Nursing and has written articles as a guest writer for the *Fort Worth Star Telegram*. Responding in a holy indignation to all the New Age nonsense on the market about angels, the theologian in Harris sought after the truth about them. The journalist in her methodically did an investigative report of what the Bible had to say about angels. The journalist and the theologian fused together to produce ANGEL CHASERS.